INDIAN CURRENCY AND EXCHANGE

INDIAN CURRENCY AND EXCHANGE

K. C. MAHINDRA

GYAN

Published by

Gyan Publishing House
5, Ansari Road
Daryaganj, New Delhi-110002
Phone: 011-47034999, 9811692060
E-mail: books@gyanbooks.com

Distribution Network
gyanbooks.com
India, USA, Canada, UK, Australia

ISBN: 978-93-7169-484-1 (PB)

First Published, 1922

2nd Impression 2025

Printed at: Gyan Press, Delhi.

INDIAN CURRENCY AND EXCHANGE
Author: K. C. MAHINDRA

INDIAN CURRENCY AND EXCHANGE

INDIAN CURRENCY AND EXCHANGE

BY

K. C. MAHINDRA, B.A. *(Cantab).*

S. GANESAN,

PUBLISHER, TRIPLICANE, MADRAS, S.E.

1922

FOREWORD

The writer owes an explanation for placing before the public this monograph on a time-old problem that has engaged the careful attention of many learned men. He does not claim the prime virtue of original merit in the following pages. His excuse for jotting down his views on a contentious subject a duty which a conscientious man will always shirk was an invitation issued by the Indian Merchants' Chamber and Bureau, Bombay, under the inspiration of Mr. S. R. Bomanji. His apology for placing it before the public is the insistent pressure of friends who feel that some good may come of it. The excuse bore fruit in the approval by the Bureau; the apology needs yet the justification.

The essay was written in July 1920 and much water has flown under the already precarious bridge of Indian currency. A prudent man would revise his judgments uttered *ex cathedra* in times when conditions were in a state of flux, but the writer feels that a revision would detract more than it would add to the value of the general fundamentals which underlie his scheme of thought. He has consequently left the text untouched. Any small change that may seem necessary because of the altered conditions to-day, occurs in the various assumptions and illustrations which he had selected for elucidation and clear thinking.

He wishes to thank in conclusion the Committee of the Indian Merchants' Chamber and Bureau for permission to publish the monograph.

6, 7 Clive Street,
CALCUTTA,
January, 1922.

K. C. MAHINDRA

CONTENTS

INDIAN CURRENCY AND EXCHANGE

INTRODUCTION

I

> "Skin for skin, yea, all that a man hath will he give for his life."

WE read this in the book of Job (ii. 4) and wonder if it conceals a currency principle. But the ancients were not a sophisticated tribe; they expressed in simple words plain matters of facts and incidents in their daily lives. Skins left over after a carnival of hunt formed a material basis of exchange and the puzzling words in the Scriptures refer to nothing more ponderous than this. Traditions record the use of leather as currency in Rome and Carthage, and even as late as the reign of Peter the Great, Russia resorted to leather for money purposes.

The use of heads of cattle as forming a convenient basis for count and proportion seems to have developed later. Homeric poems repeatedly mention oxen as the commodity in terms of which other things were valued. "The tripod, the first prize for wrestlers in the 23rd Iliad, was valued at 12 oxen and a woman captive, skilled in industry, at four!"—a blasphemy in modern days of sex equality. Carlyle has immortalised this old custom of Pecunia and oxen deserve well of us. if only for drawing out the fancy of the Chelsea sage. "A simple invention it was," says Herr Teufelsdrockh, "in the old-world Grazier—sick of lugging his slow Ox about the country till he got it bartered for Corn or Oil—to take a piece of Leather, and thereon scratch or stamp the mere Figure of an Ox (or *Pecus*), put it in his pocket, and call it Pecunia, Money. Yet hereby did Barter grow Sale, the Leather Money is now Golden and Paper, and all miracles have been out-miracled: for there are Rothschilds and English National Debts; and whoso has six pence is sovereign (to the length of six pence) over all men; commands Cooks to feed him, Philosophers to teach him, Kings to mount guard over him—to the length of six pence." * *(Sartor Resartus).*

The convenience of a common denominator of things valued or prized, was apparent to our primitive ancestors. And it was a mere accident or perhaps extra convenience that such computation was made in things visible and tangible, such as

* *C.F.* Hartley Withers: ***The Meaning of Money.***

oxen, sheep or leather and shells, Mill quotes from Montesquieu's "*Esprit des Lois*" who records that there were certain African tribes in whom value is expressed in a mere unit of calculation, in a sort of money of account, called Macutes. They say one thing is worth ten macutes, another fifteen, another twenty. There is no real thing called a Macute: it is a conventional unit for the more convenient comparison of things with one another.

What is money? I have given above three typical cases wherein men have chosen from amongst their debris of knowledge three different units of exchange—Ox as representing the live matter, leather and shells from amongst the inanimate dead world and Macute the token of an idea in the human brain. The attempt to define money, therefore, is bound to fail.

Human beings tend to conserve their efforts, the fruits of their toil and their labour, in order the better to utilise them, to drive satisfaction or pleasure therefrom, at some future period. When a workman tolls by the roadside to earn a few annas for his evening meal, he is investing human energy for a period of few hours in order to satisfy the hunger pangs which he will feel as the evening draws near. If he were to derive as much pleasure from consuming the fruits of his energy as he toiled on, as he does by withholding their consumption till it gets dark there would be no advantage in his seeking to postpone his enjoyment. That he does gather some extra utility by such conservation is the root basis of human search for a suitable medium, a receptacle which yields all that is put in it at some earlier period.

By common consent men have fixed upon money (whatever it may be!) as that receptacle which would yield approximately everything they put in it. If this "Money receptacle" has no false bottom it will give to them the equivalent of the *work* they put in. While acceptance of faith in the Money receptacle is implicit in its use, the continued preservation of faith in its virtue depends upon the treatment it metes out to its devotees.

While any money therefore will pass current if people have faith in it and if it is a convenient denominator of values, it will not sustain currency, (in its literal sense), if it is defective as a stable measure of deferred obligations. Money may be gold or silver, an ox or a shell or even a Macute, but it will not pass if it does not subserve to human standards of convenience and security. Writers of note and eminence have emphasised now one and now the other phase of good money, as the needs of the time required. Adam Smith refers to a standard of value when he writes—

> "The currency of a great state such as France and England generally consists almost entirely of it own coin."

But when Mill describes currency as a "machinery for doing quickly and commodiously what would be done though less quickly and commodiously without it", he is directing attention to the services of currency as a medium of exchange of efforts and toils and as a common measure for deferred payments. We require a full view of the picture as a whole if we desire a correct perspective. And the needs and importance of good money emphasise the value of such a viewpoint.

India shows no peculiarity or eccentricity in its needs for a good, wholesome money. She needs as much as any other country to minimise the energy required to build up an ideal "Geld-Fabrik" (the picturesque phrase of a German economist for currency mechanism). Such a Money Factory will have to be free from the ills of distemper or of unhygienic atmosphere. A harmony of interests between its various tools—its Capital and Labour—its tokens of metal or of paper is not merely essential, but the very justification of its existence is conditioned by such goodwill. A provision for automatic adjustment controls when such relations become strained, a strong tendency to secure immediate return to normal conditions of work, a sound basis of confidence in such virtues—these are few of the good old precepts for an ideal currency.

We will presently come to a detailed considera-tion of some of the specifics prescribed for Indian ills of currency. It is well to direct our analysis by the light of the fundamental issues and never to forget what money really is, what its phases of activity should be in its ideal state and how best to arrive at it with a minimum of effort. Let us note in passing what Ricardo wrote a full century back:—

> "To secure the public against any other varia-tions in the value of currency than those to which the standard itself is subject and, at the same time, to carry on the circula-tion with a medium the least expensive, is to attain the most perfect state to which a currency can be brought."

II

It is not our present purpose to present a detailed historical survey of Indian currency to date. Various Commissions and Committees in-cluding the latest have supplied us with ample material on the subject. And to arrive at an equi-table solution of the very difficult and complicated issues the present state of our currency has given rise to, it is essential to grasp a thorough experience of its past workings. While therefore we do not propose to enter into any historical review, I would like to emphasise the need of looking backwards in order the better to look forward.

It will not perhaps be out of place to mention the chief features of our currency system and I will attempt to give them in order of importance in as brief a manner as possible.

1. Rupee is our biggest coin of 180 grains of silver 11/12ths fine. It is unlimited legal tender. It is not redeemable into anything so far as law is concerned. While its value rests upon its representative character, it is a strange use to call it a token coin, for it is not small change and as recent events have shown, it is not free from dangers of exportation.

2. The English Sovereign was notified to be an unlimited legal tender at the rate of 15 rupees to £1 and was convertible at this rate. Until 1916 it was our standard of value for international exchange. Since 12th July 1920, the standard of value is changed from a sovereign to a unit of 11.30016 grains of gold. It is another matter that the standard is not effective.

3. Government strictly controls the issue of Paper money. Notes of various denominations

from one rupee upwards circulated in the country and carried on their face a promise of redeemability in Rupees at Government currency centres. This is rather important. Sir William Meyer in his evidence before the Babington Smith Committee replied to a question on inconvertibility as follows :—

> "As long as we cash paper at Government currency centres we are not inconvertible; that in fact was all our legal obligation. The previous facilities (restricted during war time) for encashment at district treasuries were a matter of grace, not of right." Q. 3132.

Our legal tender money consisted therefore of rupees and of Government currency notes not everywhere convertible into each other and not by law convertible into an exportable coin (i.e. Sovereign).

4. As a matter of administrative practice and convenience the Government would change notes and rupees into gold sovereigns but it was not a legal right you could enforce.

5. The mechanism of Council Drafts also depended upon an Executive Ordinance, and the conversion of international currency into Indian currency and *vice versa* did not effect itself automatically at the desire of the holders but rested upon the convenience of the Secretary of State for India.

6. It is often said that war time saw the breakdown of this "elastic mechanism". There was no breakdown for there was no legal obligation. The Secretary of State in his capacity of a big Banker-Trader refused to cater to the needs of the smaller fry of the same kind when a storm threatened his own stability.

7. The drift of India towards the so called Gold Exchange Standard was illusory in so far as the vital parts of the currency mechanism responded not to the needs of local and international trade but to administrative fiats issued from Whitehall or Simla. Of course the response would harmonise if the needs of Indian trade govern the interests of Whitehall and Simla, and to say that they always co-ordinated in the past is to assume certain relations which do not bear close scrutiny.

8. War effected certain changes in our currency not altogether fundamental, but those changes have revealed the true basis on which the whole structure rested. In one word, the concrete in the foundations was "Government convenience," and as the position became uncomfortable during war time and needed a shifting, the whole superstructure tumbled down only to expose the very slender bottom of our money mechanism. While embargoes were placed on the export and import of precious metals on private account, restrictions

were imposed on the transit by rail or steamer of rupees from one place to another in the country itself. The consequent rendering of immobility in internal circulation combined with the withdrawal of facilities for international settlement go to show the real fiat nature of all our money. The successive legal modifications in the Indian Paper Currency Act point to but one conclusion—Indian currency was a "managed" currency and the management was in the hands of those whose outlook was Imperial rather than Indian. The charge of "Heads I win, tails you lose" policy against the India Office wherever Indian and English—or even Colonial—interests came into conflict is not an empty one despite vehement assertions to the contrary. The evidence of Sir Lionel Abrahams and Mr. Gubbay before the Currency Committee of 1919 serves as a good eye-opener on this point. The detailed transactions of the Secretary of State with his policy of restricted Councils and "Privileged List" would be an instructive reading if they were made public. The very recent exhibition of Government Finance in the matter of sale of Reverse Councils provides another commentary in the same direction.

The present position of internal currency, then, is that Rupee never fully convertible has become incidentally an exportable coin because of the rise in the gold value of its metallic contents. Notes of various denominations from one rupee upwards have, *force majeur*, filled in the gap created by the increased demands for currency through an unprecedented rise of prices and an equally unprecedented push in the commercial activities of the country. They are practically inconvertible, or to be more strict in our phraseology, they are "not converted" in the words of Sir Lionel Abraham, the Financial Secretary to the India Office. There has been alongside a heavy absorption of rupees, explained by the denial of the usual facilities for obtaining bullion —both gold and silver—for social and industrial purposes. The effective embargo on the import and export of the precious metals imposed evidently under direct orders from the British Treasury eventually brought about a condition of things which in the opinion of the India Office could only be solved by a Committee of experts. The difficulties of circulation accentuated the accumulation of bad spots which in the normal course of things usually disappear through the regular flow of the stream.

International trade has come in for its share of the ills. The restriction on the limits of Councils, the Approved List, the secret arrangement with a few of the favoured houses, the policy of silver purchase, the overstepping the limits of safety in the matter of the metallic reserves, the subordination of the Indian Finance, in a word, to the needs of the London Money Market--all these have contributed to a disharmony in the normal course of India's trade with other countries, England not excepted. While Indian export trade has complained grievously for want of finance and cover, the imports were handicapped by war conditions in Europe and the extra patriotic License system introduced in India. The Babington Smith recommendations were accepted by the Government of India in February 1920 and their first way to "get at 'em" was the sale of Reverse Councils! I will not use any stronger word than is absolutely necessary and justified by events; but since the Government of India have not till to-day (July 19th 1920) seen the unwisdom and the folly of such a sale, it is pardonable perhaps to reserve our opinion on it and place it in the category of so many other exhibitions of Whitehall finance which do not explain themselves. Witness the difficulties and the impasse we find ourselves in to-day and Prof. Nicholson's indictment of British War Finance becomes no less applicable to India :—

> "In the actual conduct of the war we have acknowledged and amended great mistakes. . . . . In diplomacy also we erred, repented and reformed. . . . .

> But in regard to our economic and financial policy no mistakes are admitted . . . . . . Granted, that from a balancing of various causes some rise in prices was probable and some extravagance unavoidable, it is foolish to say that none of the causes are under human control and that we must go on in the way we have begun."
>
> "In fact the Government has struck the snag of *too much*. Its emergency measures have gone too far and been continued too long."

III

What then is the real nature of problem? There is a vast confusion in the innumerable treatments which have been made of the disease. The confusion has been to a certain extent inevitable; the fundaments lie hidden under a tangled mass of immediate side issues which required a direct attention. The mind was focussed on particulars whereas the general basic maladjustments remained unnoticed and unrepaired. But such attempts, in themselves partial and limited, while effecting little or nothing, lead to a grievous misunderstanding and block the way to a just appreciation. I must admit, however, that granting the limited hypotheses, some of them are brilliant expositions of one aspect of the problem; but when we mistake them for a solution of the whole we tend rather to get away from the centrics of the problem. Instances occur to me in very large numbers and it will be invidious to specify them. However I might mention the expert opinion on the subject and take Sir Lionel Abraham's suggestions as a case in point. Sir Lionel's diagnosis of the situation refers to three main problems:—(i) whether the rate of exchange is to be a fixed one or a variable one?—(ii) If a variable rate is to be allowed, should the mints remain closed as they have been since 1893?—and (iii) Under what conditions should the sale of Councils be carried on? (Memorandum B)

Now to assert that these are the only three main problems before us is either to confuse ignorance with stolidity or contemptuously insult the economic knowledge of the reader. I mean no prejudice to Sir Lionel. He would perhaps, by some trick of sophistry, include any other more important issue you may put forward under his three headings and make you look silly in your questionnairs. But to face the issue honestly, is there any talk of the general level of prices in India? Is there even the slightest hint of the Gold question which Sir William Meyer called the "Alpha and the Omega of the Indian Currency difficulties"? Are any problems of internal currency to be considered under these headings? Did Sir Lionel consider the question of economic suitability of the currency as a pertinent problem, or is it merely ancillary to his third group? I am afraid words will have to be stretched a good deal in their meanings to include these and various other issues in his categories and the examination of Sir Lionel before the Committee bears me out in this particular respect.

Let us turn to Mr. Gubbay's distinctions. While in "the Government of India's statement, the problem as it appears to them is the consideration of the means of securing the greatest practical stability of the rupee in the terms of the sovereign", Mr. Gubbay would rather put it in this way, that "really the problem is, to what extent the interests of trade should be made to depend upon currency necessities or whether currency should not be regarded as subservient to trade." Q. 390.

Now while the Government of India rigorously directed attention to one and but one of the main issues, Mr. Gubbay's analysis might mean anything and nothing. While it is easy to understand that if trade interests are considered supreme, stability of exchange value of the rupee becomes an essential factor, it is not so easy to follow to the logical end the other line, viz., when currency necessities are to rule the policy. Mr. Gubbay might have meant to convey nothing or he may have been hinting at the vast problems of inconvertibility, of token money, of metallic Reserves. But surely these are also of equal concern to trade in the long run and Mr. Gubbay's fine distinction and the thesis built upon it would seem to hint at a not very definite approach to the real problem.

Finally, we find the Babington Smith Committee devoting practically the whole of their time in discovering the causes and effects of a high exchange rate of the rupee. They no doubt gave a serious thought to the problem of general prices in India but the argument proceeded from a very artificial basis. International trade and international standards of comforts do not depend on the particular counters that are used for facilitating the exchange. Their measure and their content rise above the fineness or the weight of the unit of account. A tinkering of the medium of exchange —which is merely a facility—does not increase or diminish the quantum of real goods and services which a country provides. Human work put in the production or consumption of a whole country is in no way related, for its degree of intensity, to the particular counters in use at any particular time. There is no "*deus ex machina*" by which a mere administrative fiat like raising or lowering the contents of the currency could increase the real wealth of the country. It is an excess of solicitude for the facility and convenience of foreign trade interests to devote all your attention to solving a particular and limited side issue and without any reference to the bases of the problem.

In my judgment the problem of all currency is the problem of *good money.* We have chosen an ingenious device for our convenience and we should naturally wish it to efficiently perform its functions. If it is a question of fluctuating foreign exchange rate, what we have really to enquire is not whether it hinders or promotes the immediate interests of a section of the trade, but rather the pivotal issue whether a variable rate of exchange introduces any disharmonies in the general price level in the country; whether our commitments of trust in the solid foundations of the money receptacle are perfectly honoured, i.e., whether our money is a real, active standard for our deferred obligations, our postponed enjoyments, our anxieties for future investments of our toil and energy? We have heard a lot of the gold issue and the silver issue. But gold and silver are accidental representatives of our notions about exchange of goods and services. We had to choose something; we stumbled on the precious metals after our experience with shells and leather, oxen and perhaps Macutes. The gold or silver problem does not stand by itself: it is actively subordinate to the primary necessities of a good money.

and so must realise itself through a fulfilment of the attributes of good money.

I have called my first problem, the stability problem in currency, and it is discussed in details in its bearings on the present Indian currency in its proper place. But it will be advisable to dispose of certain preliminary objections. The chief feature in money values I would look for when contracting a debt, is if at the time of discharge I will be paying the same back, or more or less. Suppose I can enjoy a hundred Macutes (a Macute being any self-constituted unit) of pleasure by at once consuming the fruits of my toil for one hour. And if by postponing my consumption for one week I could enjoy 120 Macutes worth by the same initial outlay of toil, I will agree to such a postponement. If during the interval of this week a sort of brain wave halves the pleasure unit of Macute so that whereas one Macute would have sufficed before, now two Macutes do the same work, I have every reason and argument to complain of the vagaries of the brain wave which have given me only 60 Macutes worth of pleasure after a week while I conserved a 100 units in anticipation of obtaining 120 Macutes worth. It is therefore desirable that the Macutes should be above interference from brain waves, that is, our unit of account should be stable in its value. This is agreed and beyond any grave dispute.

But what exactly does. stability mean? How should we measure it, is perhaps a more definite criterion of its definition. Currency has had its poets and an ingenious person glorified the puzzle of stability in a doggeral poem published in England in 1811---during the famous Paper Pound period. Our poet classified the various conceptions of currency. The man in the street accepted the pound, the shilling and the pence. To the bankers the circulation of notes appeared as the barometer of the money market, for money issued in "best paper" could not be issued beyond the requirements of the trade. But

> "In Francis Burleigh's head
> The real test was a loaf of bread."

This emphasises the proletarian point of view. The price of bread---the food of the millions---formed the representative criterion of stability.

> "While Adam Smith did always say
> That it was the labour of the day."

The real test of stability was the return of the same labour which we originally invested in the money receptacle. This is the only logical standard. Ricardo adopted it and Prof. Marshall has followed him up as will be clear from his evidence before the Indian Currency Committee of 1898-99:—

> "A person who borrows a peck of green peas in April and returns two pecks in June, has paid no interest at all, he has not even returned the corpus of the loan."

The real value of money is its power of purchasing not commodities but labour of all kinds—that is, not only manual labour, but the labour of business men and all others engaged in industry of any kind. This test is hotly denied by other writers of eminence, among them Professors Cannon and Foxwell of London University. Their objections are valid enough so long as reference is made to the expediency of currency legislation for the purpose. For instance, what does labour actually consist of?—Skilled or unskilled, six hour machinist or the ten hour docker and so on. How shall we construct the actual index number? These are practical difficulties in our way of accepting the labour test of stability as a working hypothesis. But from the social standard point of view, the only logical stand is on the labour value basis. It is not our present purpose to enter into the theory of the argument.

In matters of daily practice the powers of purchasing labour and commodities respectively synchronise for a particular period and we will not gain any appreciable advantage in adopting the line of cleavage. Ultimately labour goes in to produce all commodities. So by the stability problem in currency we will mean the problem of the purchasing power in commodities of our particular counter.

The second subdivision I have adopted refers to our foreign trade obligations. It is the problem of the Gold Standard Reserve, of economy and facility in our trade transactions with other countries. The question of the sale of Councils has loomed large before the Smith Committee and Sir L. Abraham raised the issue to the dignity of a problem by itself. The policy of restricted sale of drafts to a favoured few during war time had evoked large criticism from people who thought they suffered an injury; and perhaps the truth in the charge provoked India Office in the person of its Financial Secretary to a detailed defence. And Sir Lionel, forced in defence of his honesty of purpose, elaborated the issue into an unnecessary prominence. Councils come in our mechanism of currency as mitigators or reducers of friction whenever an excess of exports over imports makes India a creditor country for the nonce. If there were no Councils, the fact of credit would remain which would be settled by payments of international currency to India in the form she liked. There are other equally important issues besides the sales of Council drafts, issues which refer to our gold problem, to the question of our foreign credits, to our financial standing amongst the nations of the earth. I have restricted my heading to the problem of the Gold Standard Reserve, for, as a matter of actual fact, that reserve is the only foreign credit we can boast of now. Our ability to create foreign credits is denied by the experts, under the rather questionable hypothesis that India needs all the capital she can lay her hands on and therefore she could not afford an outlay in foreign countries. Whatever amount of truth there be in this assertion —it can be either accepted or denied, there is no other way about it—what matters us really more is the careful husbanding of our foreign credits whatever they are now. The Gold Standard Reserve may not be a necessary adjunct of the plan we may eventually suggest, but it will certainly form the basis of any modification that may be considered desirable for our foreign financial arrangements.

The third and the final problem I have named the Elasticity problem. By Elasticity I mean the power of automatic expansion and contraction under a well directed force. India perhaps above all other big countries shows a peculiarity in the abnormal variations in her seasonal demands for currency for internal circulation. In no other country the vagaries of monsoon control to such a large extent the movement of and demands for currency. And so far as barometric variations are beyond the control of human laws, the money of India will continue to be exposed to a large range of uncontrolled forces and thereby necessitate a very large provision of resilience in the currency issue. The problem of note issue, its metallic and fiduciary backing, the proper disposition of such reserves—all these issues come under this head. To a certain extent the question of currency circulation in the country touches the border lines of our first problem. The gold and silver issue we will discuss under our first problem of stability and its bearings on the internal money directly we will leave for our final section. Then again India has been made notorious as a sink for precious metals. The general truth about hoards is not sufficiently known and we will attempt to explain the true nature of the hoards and how they stand in relation to the demands for precious metals for currency purposes and for social and domestic uses respectively.

Before we enter on our detailed analysis I would

plead for a consideration of the problem in toto and not piecemeal. The necessities of analysis would compel us to put it into bits and attempt a reconstruction on that basis, but unless the bits fit into a harmonious whole, the attempt will be to a large extent futile. In presenting therefore the threefold aspects of the problem we have been guided all along by the oneness of the issue; there is a unity running along all the complicated threads which we pick up here and there for examination. So also in our synthesis the master force has been the attempt to arrive ultimately at a *good* money.

Finally most of our work perhaps will sound commonplace and obvious and many of our observations as mere truisms. But a truism is not quite the same thing as a home truth which mankind accepts in *foro conscientiae,* but ignores in practice. This is my chief apology for and incentive to laying stress on the obvious and the patent.

STABILITY PROBLEM IN CURRENCY

"Without stability of value money is a fraud."
G. Poulett Scrope.

The problem of stability of currency presents as varied and complex an issue as the akin subject of stability of ships. Abnormal events come unforeseen in both cases and disaster overtakes the best scientifically constructed base. An economic hurricane may throw the best currency machine out of gear as swiftly and rapidly as a sudden gale may endanger our biggest liners. Stability conveys the idea of evenness in motion. It is equilibrium not only under static conditions but we imply what perhaps may be called a dynamic equilibrium—a conception not unfamiliar in mathematics. A currency is stable if the value of the purchasing power of a unit remains steady over a period. Exchange is stable if the value of the currency unit in terms of the similar units of a foreign country remains the same over a period. We have to distinguish thus between a stable currency and a stable exchange. Perhaps some people would term this distinction as mere hair-splitting and with no difference. But a study of the very abnormal fluctuations in the Indian Exchange combined with the proportionately much narrow range of fluctuations in the local purchasing power of the rupee will demonstrate the vital difference and the great value to be attached to this distinction. The exchange value of the rupee has hovered round the central figure 1s. 4d. from 1898 onwards till the outbreak of hostilities. It would postulate, if no distinction be made between rupee stability and exchange stability, that the price line in India has moved in the same direction and approximately to the same degree as in England. The following table gives the general index number of prices for 39 selected articles for India and also the Sauerbeck index for United Kingdom :—

COMPARATIVE INDEX NUMBERS—INDIA AND UNITED KINGDOM

(Average of 1867-77 being 100)

YEAR	INDIA General Index Number: 28 Exported and 11 Imported Articles	UNITED KINGDOM Sauerbeck Index Number: 45 Articles
1894	101	63
95	103	62
96	109	61
97	112	62
98	95	64
99	95	68
1900	115	75
1	109	70
2	105	69
3	98	69
4	100	70
5	109	72
6	128	77
7	136	80
8	137	73
9	123	74
1910	121	78
11	128	80
12	136	85
13	142	85
14	146	85

We find as a matter of fact that the parallelism is not only not apparent but ceases altogether at various stages. No doubt we can explain the cause of it, but that does not obviate the need of a distinction between the two sorts of stability.

A certain number of disingenuous people labour under the mistake that provided we attain a fixity of exchange we will automatically obtain certainty in the economic affairs of this life. Fixity of exchange value of currency never means fixity of the purchasing power and if, what I contend, is right, that is, the purchasing power stability is the only real problem, the fixity of exchange must remain secondary to our first obligation. Indeed, as Sir L. Abraham puts it in his Memorandum "B" submitted to the Currency Committee:—

> "The experience of the past half century is that in India steadiness in the real value of money has been assisted rather by instability than by stability in the rate of exchange with gold standard countries."

From 1873–93 Indian prices index number varied within sixteen per cent and prices in 1893 were only 5% higher than in 1873. On the other hand price-range in United Kingdom showed a fluctuation of 39%—the biggest change was represented in the year 1893 when prices were 39% less than what they were in 1873.

The difference therefore in the two stabilities is very real. Why people refuse to bother about such distinctions and prejudice their minds by dismissing the subject as merely academic, is aptly described by Prof. Cannon as "the consequence of their being so habitually accustomed to measure values by money that they feel towards any suggestion that the value of money itself wants measuring just as the aged villager feels towards the suggestion that the distance between two milestones from which he has throughout life taken his idea of a mile is 50 yards short." We admit that under certain conditions the two stabilities harmonise, but we must be careful about the premiss. I have the high authority of the eminent Swedish economist, G. Cassel in support. He says:—

> "The real parity between two countries is represented by the quotient between the internal purchasing power against goods of the money of each country. . . . .
> I propose to call this parity "the purchasing power parity". As long as anything like free movement of merchandise and a somewhat comprehensive trade between the two countries takes place, the actual

> rate of exchange cannot deviate very much from this purchasing power parity ".

Exception was taken to Dr. Cassel's theory, viz., that movements of the exchanges are simply determined in the main by the quotient between the inflation of the different countries, on the ground that the theory does not explain the very abnormal and curious tricks that exchanges have played during war time. Hence we believe Dr. Cassel's qualification as in the last sentence of the paragraph quoted above. Perhaps it may be added for a completer elucidation that two further reservations are necessary in the same connection, namely, (i) the two countries have a simlar monetary basis—not necessarily gold, and (ii) there is a free movement of this monetary measure.

Dr. Cassel illustrates in support the Swedish experience. In 1918 the approximate figure for Swedish inflation was 330, while English figure according to the *Economist's* index was 250 as against 100 before the war. And yet the sterling rate of exchange was quoted at about 14 crowns as against 18·16 crowns as the old mint parity! The explanation seems to be, according to him, the exceedingly severe restrictions on Swedish imports. I may add to it the probably significant effects of the closing up of the free gold market; of the severance of Swedish currency from its old base, gold, in 1916; and the artificial complexities of the war situation.

In the Indian Exchange history too we notice the artificial divorce consistently kept up till 1916 between the exchange parity and the purchasing-power parity. We looked with anxiety at the recent jumps in the exchange value of the rupee which betokened the failure of the Government to maintain exchange stability. And now when Rupee fluctuates chiefly according to its metallic contents it may be augured that exchange parity and purchasing-power parity will 'tend to harmonise. But we ignore the restrictions placed on the import and export of precious metals which hindered to a very large extent this harmonising tendency.

We should also note that although in the ultimate run because of growing interdependence of international trade the world price-levels at sea-ports may tend to run parallel, but at any given moment the difference between the local price-level and the price-gradation represented by foreign indebtedness is mathematically significant.

So when we are considering the problem of stabilising the rupee we mean by it the problem presented by the fluctuations in the purchasing-power of a rupee in terms of the local commodities-in-general. A general reading however of the elixirs prescribed by our economic doctors shows that by stability of the Rupee they mean stability of the Indian exchange. In my opinion the false nomenclature is to a certain extent responsible for the very halting difficulties that the various proposals suffer from. We will come to this confusion later. There is also the difference between temporary makeshifts to ease a particular situation and permanent props needed to secure a sound structure. It would add to clear thinking if these preliminary but vital distinctions be kept in mind and due reservations made for their interrelational-effects.

To revert to our general argument of the stability problem the first point that needs consideration is the desirability or otherwise of currency stability with reference to the general economic welfare of the country. The question assumes a more intelligible shape if we put it like this: which of the two —rising or falling prices—is beneficial for the economic progress of a nation? There are three aspects of economic progress—Productive, Distributive and Selective. By the last we mean the general standard of living of the people (the word selective has been chosen because of the lack of any other more expressive word). We will consider them one by one. But we must assume, to start with, that industrial conditions remain stationary. It is a purely monetary effect we are seeking to analyse and the super-imposition of an extraneous cause like, say, famine or war, may retard or even turn back the original monetary effect. It is essential therefore to assume that only the currency force is at work.

A. Any effect on Production will be reflected in the national dividend of the country. A regime of rising prices introduces a flutter of expectation of higher profits to the trading public. They form the principal debtor class in the country and so gain in the event of a rise in price level. With a cheerful optimism backed by a greater power of foreseeing immediately future events, the merchant class freely makes bigger investments. Impetus is given to old industries and a start is made possible for new ones. *Prima facie* therefore National Dividend stands to gain from rising price. But this is not all. Under the rising wing of cheap prosperity firms which were with difficulty dragging along their existence, gain a fresh lease of life. So far as they are encouraged to prolong their wasteful life, they produce a worsening effect on the future character of the national dividend. Merchants and traders are content to reap big profits with little trouble and there is no impelling motive to continue in those ever improving habits which create a tradition and a permanence of industrial superiority.

While the selective force of competition is rendered very much feeble during times when everybody is flushed with prospects of higher prices, the premium on incompetency which rising prices yield reacts grievously upon the economic prosperity of the nation. Wild, insecure schemes are fopped upon the public. The unscrupulous do not hesitate to bring down to a crash the house they have taken shelter under and profited thereby; but they generally take care to get out of it before the disaster falls.

When prices are falling, Prof. Marshall writes, "everybody who undertakes a business risk is likely to have his risks turn out worse than if prices were rising. . . . . Many business men strike . . . . there are some exceptional failures". But this never lasts long. A period of falling prices puts the manufacturer on his mettle and incites him to search for better and more efficient methods of production. We find the money market get timid and people with a command over the loan fund much more cautious in their investments than under a spell of rising prices. While the incompetents are pushed out the intellectual energy put forth in the management of capital is maximised to the ultimate benefit of the National Dividend.

We have the considered judgment of Prof.

Marshall: "One wants very much stronger statistical evidence than one yet has to prove that a fall of prices diminishes perceptibly and in the long run the total productiveness of industry."

So far as the National Dividend is concerned, there are no outstanding advantages in either case. The tendencies in one direction seem to be balanced by contrary movements in other directions.

B. In considering the Distributive aspect we have to note first, whether any change is effected at all in relative social nature of distribution of the national dividend by such monetary changes, and secondly whether such shiftings harmonise with the progressive tendencies of the people as a whole.

A priori, a fall in prices is advantageous, for it means more commodities with the same income to work-people who form by far the greatest part of the population of a country. There will be a tendency for wages to come down but it is a well known fact that they lag behind all movements in prices. But this is not the total effect. A period of falling prices means a dislocation of industrial activities, a contraction of the occupational sphere and a consequent greater degree of unemployment. Statistics are very meagre on this point. Prof. Bowley's summary of the course of money wages prices and real wages during XIX century for United Kingdom is both interesting and instructive :—

Periods	*Nominal Wages*	*Prices*	*Real Wages*
1810-30	Falling	Falling fast	Rising slow
1830-52	Stationary	„ slow	do
1852-70	Rising fast	Rising	Rising considerably
1870-73	„ very fast	„ fast	Rising fast
1873-79	Falling fast	Falling fast	Stationary
1879-87	Stationary	Falling	Rising
1887-92	Rising	Rising & falling	do
1892-97	Stationary	Falling	do
1897-1900	Rising fast	Rising	do

Prof. Bowley's table can be taken as representing not even a tendency but a mere drift—there are so many other causes at work that monetary influences share but a part of the total force. And this fact explains many a departure we find from the *prima facie* effects we should expect from a fall or rise in prices. Statistics do not give us any big help, for isolation of one cause from others is pretty nearly impossible. What we can safely generalise from these movements is that rising prices with scarcity are bad while falling prices plus abundance and good harvests produce good effects.

Against the benefit to wage earners of a fall in prices we have to put the uncalculated force of custom and habit which makes people buy "at the next corner." When prices shift about, the retail shop keepers do not in a hurry alter their lists and so far the workmen clients do not obtain the benefits of falling prices. This is true only for a short period. Ultimately prices must shift to the newer level. In spite of these obstructive tendencies of customary prices and unemployment there seems to be solid ground for believing that during a period of falling prices the workman class benefits at the expense of the merchant manufacturers, and this is a net social gain.

C. What effect shifting prices have on the general standard of living of the people? The selective principle amongst nations is a long time effect. People with an increasing level of standard can afford to bear better and for a longer period the strain which the struggle for racial exploitation produces. The forces that tend to uplift the standard of living act in a number of different ways under varying kinds of stress. We have seen that while rising prices serve to create a flutter, a ripple on the surface of productive activity, they tend to produce an impression of optimism in industrial circles. And so far as new wants are deliberately created for the consumption of the prospective supplies which will come on the market, the average man stands for a better standard of living. It may be that such created wants may be thoroughly inimical to ultimate betterment, but that will imply a defective strain in the national stock. At the same time the great handicap that is put on the wage earners during this period of rising prices. serves to degrade the general standard of living to a mere saturation of physical needs. We can on the other hand argue that with a greater command over commodities and service, during falling prices, an average citizen will tend to devote part of his increased powers towards real betterment--an argument that has recently been testified to by a series of studies made amongst the Miners of South Wales who with increased wages invariably invested a part of them in buying pianos and clean collars for their boys.

On the whole therefore we have not much to choose between rising and falling prices. What has emerged out of this discussion is the fact of steady prices as the result of monetary stability as being wholly beneficial to economic welfare and as superior to both rising and falling prices. We should make it clear at this stage that only long time effects were considered. A sudden rise or a sudden fall in prices is wholly injurious to all sections of the community and we must not mistake such sudden injuries as the result of a particular monetary change. They are not monetary evils at large but in fact social maladies which come at the top of serious maladjustments in the economic balance.

How far our arguments are seriously affected by the particular case of India requires only a brief mention, for the exceptions are few. We have referred to the growing timidity of capital during a period of falling prices; in India this timidity would shrink into positive abstinence at the signal of reduced profits. But the effect would not be due to purely economic reasons. Political and social dangers of insecurity influenced largely in the past our big capitalists; but it is a sign of the coming times that such differences will soon be obliterated by growing inter-relationship between India and foreign countries.

Then again the position of the ryot, the biggest factor of Indian population, is peculiar in itself. Rising prices bring good profits to producers. The agricultural ryot is a producer, but he will hardly gain from the rise: he is seriously indebted to the local moneylender and the tribute he pays is more often in kind, uninfluenced by any price level. The tribute is so large that barely a sustenance is left over to him. Mr. K. L. Datta in his evidence before the Currency Committee asserted that the "bulk of the profits (accrued from high prices during war time) has gone into the pockets of the middleman and the exporter". He instanced the case of jute: the rise in price of raw jute was insignificant as compared to the rise in price of gunnies and hessians. The index numbers fully bear out his statement. Agricultural interests do not therefore gain much from a rise in the prices of their stuff. And they are so poor here in India that hardly any other change in the prices of other commodities, except possibly piece-goods, affect the debt-ridden tenant. His consumption articles are limited to a very small number and it is the comparative shifting of prices within this range which affects his gain or loss. So far the case of India is peculiar. Her poverty combines with her "low nerve tension" (in the words of Sir Stanley Reed) to make it imperative that her power of resistance should be strengthened and means towards bettering the average standard of living adopted. For the latter object all fluctuations of prices are bad: with a steadiness in the purchasing power of currency, the country will set out towards achieving command over mechanical and natural resources which will increase her national dividend and conserve for her the energy for profitable employment which she would otherwise waste in balancing now one side, then the other of an alternating fluctuation in the price level.

Mr. J. M. Keynes, although a redoubtable advocate of the so called gold exchange standard, pointed to the only real solution of India's currency *malaise*, when he said in his evidence :—

> "I should aim always . . . . . . at keeping Indian prices stable in relation to commodities rather than in relation to any particular metallic or particular foreign currency. That seems to me of far greater importance to India". Q. 2690.

II

We have attempted to state our first proposition in a form that could stand no controversion : stability in the purchasing power of money is the ideal all monetary systems unconsciously work for to attain. Almost as a direct follow-up from this proposition is the question of exchanges. In the classic words of Goschen, exchanges are an "unerring mercantile and monetary barometer . . . they are at once the necessary result and certain index of the inequalities which exist in the indebtedness of different countries, inequalities either in the amount of their liabilities or in the time within which payment must be made or in the relation of the currency of one country to that of another." The last clause is pertinent to the problem in hand. The disturbance in one particular equilibrium position of foreign exchanges due to changes in the international value of the currency of one country stirs up a score of effects in the economic life of the nation. A judicious appreciation of such effects would justify or condemn the monetary change in the standard.

We have witnessed during the last four years a progressively high rupee exchange, and the question whether it has been beneficial or otherwise to the country has become vital again. Whereas before the closing of the mints in 1893 a depreciating rupee formed the pivot of policy, the position is now reversed. Herschell Committee of 1893 gave full consideration to the effects of a depreciating currency on the producing and the consuming interests and it scarcely seemed open to further dispute—the opinion was so conclusive and well considered. But recent discussions in India and some evidence tendered before the Babington Smith Committee show that the exact bearings of the question are not yet fully understood. Before we start on a resurvey of the present position of exchange, we must note and constantly bear in mind that all exchange is elaborated barter of goods and services. The facts of import and export indicate the relative needs and relative costs of commodities (including gold and silver) and of services in transit. And that the incidental use of one commodity as money merely complicates but never alters the true ratio of gain to effort, for the money-commodity because of its position as such comes to command an unlimited world market which few other commodities can boast of, and that is the chief change introduced by the intervention of a counter in our barter transaction.

Does a rise in the exchange value of the rupee permanently alter the foreign trade relations of India? It has been suggested that the effect of the rise is a serious permanent handicap to Indian exporting interests and a sort of a bounty to the English importer into India. There is a risk of big confusion on this point and I will attempt to show the two sides of the case with their full bearing on the ultimate interests of India.

A change in the exchange value of the rupee from 1s. 4d. to 2s. means that for every pound sterling worth of goods exported from India, the trader will obtain Rs. 10 instead of Rs. 15. There is a *prima facie* check to exports and on equally strong incentive to the English merchant to send goods to India; the latter obtains an increasing number of pounds to every rupee worth of stuff sold in India. The following illustration is suggested as making clear the actual way the high exchange works. The produce of a certain wheat field in India fetches £100 at the level of 1s. 4d. to the rupee when exported. The producing interests obtain for this Rs. 1500/- in India; with 2s. rupee they will be getting only Rs. 1000/-. Perhaps the claims on his particular production by way of costs, wages, Government cess and interest amounted to Rs. 1200/-. The rising of the exchange would turn a gain of Rs. 300/- into a loss of Rs. 200/-. He will have no interest or desire to go on exporting. On the other hand, the English textile merchant can now obtain for 100 yards of piece-goods, on which he has spent the same "costs" as before, one and half times the number of pounds that he obtained before when rupee was equivalent to 1s. 4d. It is said that this tremendous advantage to the English importer goes towards competing out the Indian textile producer, and with the automatic drop in exports, combines to react injuriously to the material interests of India all round. Instances have been given of the striking way such a change in the exchanges reacts. Prof. Kemerer gives a Hakodate illustration where a renewal of a contract for supply of pipes by an English firm had to fall through because of the great depreciation of the Hakodate dollar during the interval between the first and the second contract. In 1892 when the first tender was accepted each ton weight of pipes cost four guineas or 28 silver dollars. In 1894 the tender price offered by the same firm was four sovereigns per ton—a lowering of 5% in gold value. But the silver dollar had risen to the parity of 10 dollars to one sovereign and 40 dollars were required in 1894 to buy one ton of pipes which cost 28 dollars in 1892. The consequence was a refusal of the tender —a check to imports into Hakodate because of its depreciated currency. The view was very widely held in the years when silver was depreciating. The Mexican Monetary Commission of 1903 arrived at the unanimous conclusion that "Mexico had been expending a growing proportion of her labour and intellectual efficiency in return for a given amount of foreign products" (during a period of falling Mexican Peso) and this was due in part to the monetary system.

Now this effect of a depreciating currency giving a fillip to the exports formed a subject of acute grievance to the European exporter of goods. Witness the various commissions from 1883 to 1898 which examined this question in its various aspects. Now the position is reversed. It is the Indian exporter who squeals and adduces in his favour the oft repeated arguments of olden days of controversy. While he personally suffers a material loss in not scoring off so many rupees as before, the vantage position in which his English rival is placed in the home market adds to a personal loss the grievous sense of exploitation. There is a good deal of truth in these *prima facie* direct effects, but some confusion has arisen because of the impatience of man to ignore the ultimates in favour of the immediately visible reactions.

It is a simple arithmetic of calculation which tells us that if the prices in India remain fixed, a fall in the value of pound sterling of 10% increases the gross receipts of the English exporter to India by 10%. With 10% increased funds in sterling the English produce for the purpose of exportation to India will be stimulated. Compared to him the Indian producer feels a handicap by the exchange rise. Now this is true so far as first effects go. But this advantage to the English producer will remain even if he were producing for home consumption and to say that rise in exchange value of rupee gives a bounty to English exporting interests is not a clear way of expressing the real position. For to quote the classic words of Prof. Marshall who disposed of this argument conclusively before "The Gold and Silver Commission of 1888"...." There was a *petitio principii* in the argument; the conclusion arrived at was unconsciously glided into the argument".

it is of course perfectly true that with a rise in exchange imports into India will be stimulated, if we suppose that the rise in exchange has not been accompanied by any changes in prices; but then it is of the nature of the case that that it will be so accompanied. . . . . The argument is like this: - "If a man is in the cabin of a ship only 10 feet high and the ship sinks down 12 feet in a trough, his head will be broken against the roof of the cabin. This argument implicitly assumes that when the ship falls he will not fall." And Mr. Manu Subedar in his evidence is reported to have said: "I regard the stoppage of exports at top prices which could be realised for export commodities as a great injury to the country, because it prevents the acquisition of wealth to India which would otherwise be possible." Q. 3537.

It is implied in this protest that the export merchant could have, but for the folly of raising the exchange, brought extra wealth to the country. Perhaps at the particular period the rise of rupee exchange hindered his operations, the conditions of his netting a good profit were favourable, but to say that his normal powers of bringing in more real wealth to India without paying out more involves as in Prof. Marshall's instance, a *petitio principii* in the argument.

The elemental cause of confusion on this point

is our readiness to forget the real nature of international trade. It is simply an exchange of commodities for commodities—a gigantic barter of which the modern parallel is to be found in the recently formed Swiss "Goods Exchange Centre." England will not send more goods to India unless India sends more in return, unless of course there has occured an independent cause altering the relative costs of production. There is no charity in trade. It is as hard a taskmaster as the inexorable law of gravitation and always exacts its "pound of flesh". If a purely monetary cause like rise in the exchange value of rupee gives a fillip to import trade, as it certainly does to start with, there will be more imported goods in the Indian market. The exports being checked the glut will tend to overtax the demand and an adjustment of prices all along the line will be necessary for a restoration of the equilibrium level. If this new level shows a permanent alteration, the cause must be sought for in influences other than mere currency manipulation, for any new position of equilibrium would mean an altered relation of the goods imported and exported. A change in the relative values of pound and rupee, that is, in the relative values of gold and silver can have no influence on the price of cottons relatively to other commodities. Then again we must note that a rise in exchange value of rupee does not always mean a stimulus to the English importer, howsoever temporary. Conditions can be conceived in which an incentive may be given instead to the export trade by a rise in the exchange value of the rupee. Suppose, for instance, the rupee is a full valued standard coin, as it practically was from 1916 onwards and suppose also that there is a great scarcity in India of the metal of which the rupee is made, the effect will be reflected in a premium on the rupee. This will tend to raise its exchange value, but will mean not a stimulus to the English merchant who sends goods here, but, on the contrary, a sort of a bonus to the export trade of India. The tendency will be to attract as much silver from outside to India as they can in order to avail of the premium obtained in India and this tendency will show itself in an increased spurt to the export trade.

We have thus to recognise that any bounty or stimulus that an English merchant will receive in the long run because of the rise in exchange value of rupee, will be quite independent of his exports to India. If he were producing for home trade, he would gain as much, for the cause lies in the depreciation of his sterling currency. It is quite natural that the Indian exporter will look with envy at the easier paths of his English competitor whose wages bill and costs expenses remain stationary while his receipts for the time being are increased. But the English merchant's favourable position is first, independent of the fact that he produces for export and secondly his gain is made at the expense partly of his capitalist financiar but mainly of his employees. As the gain proceeds from a depreciation of his own currency, the old wage rate will not suffice to go round for an average worker to buy his customary necessities. There will soon occur a shifting of wage level, an adjustment all along the line. So far as the producer can retard this tendency, he will gain. But this has nothing to do with the appreciation of rupee exchange. Then again the gain is of the exporting houses, the entrepreneurs of trade. We cannot regard their interests as co-extensive with those of the whole trade. They are middle-men and their services not altogether indispensible; they do not form the backbone of all trade which is production.

We have also to consider the social value of such gains or losses. The shiftings are from one class to another and we hold that so long as the wage earners do not suffer any lowering of their real wage rate, that is, so long as all shiftings are in their favour the result will be a gain on the whole to the net amount of the National Dividend. If the

Indian merchant is prevented, through a rise in the exchange, from exploiting his employees, we consider it to be a beneficient tendency. I must not be understood to mean that a nation should resort to such tinkerings of her exchange value as happen to benefit the wage-earning class. It is the effect of a particular cause we are considering and if we find in its sphere of influence one beneficient tendency, this is not enough argument to insist on the converse proposition. The one great obstacle to the acceptance of our principles of exchange transactions is the relative differences in the nature of production in India and in Europe. While it is broadly termed capitalistic in the latter case, India is mainly an agricultural country and her exports consist mostly of food grains and raw materials. The fact of the "industry" in India being agricultural and not capitalistic introduces certain halting disharmonies in the natural course of events. While on the one hand the merchant middleman assumes all the functions of a trader without the responsibilities of production, on the other, the course of adjustment of prices takes a longer and more difficult path than would be the case if Indian production were largely capitalistic. "The vast injury to the export trade" is the whip dog of the merchant as he squeals at every rise in rupee exchange and the ryots' interests are a convenient peg to hang his own business losses. Then the retarding influence of custom in opposing price changes was reflected in a continuation of the conditions which gave an advantage to the foreign merchant. But it is easy to overestimate the force of custom. There is no doubt a marked difference in the movements of price line in India and in United Kingdom, but the cause is other than the obstructive force of custom. In case of commodites whose prices are controlled by world conditions such as wheat and cotton, Indian prices follow the world prices and the average price of such exports keeps close to the general movements of English prices expressed in silver. So these little peculiarites of India do not controvert the conclusion arrived at under a more generalised hypothesis: that "nations do not make presents to one another. They do borrow and they do lend; and the dislocations between the exports and the imports, seem to be all due either to a change in the relations of borrowing or lending, or to a change in the character of the services and goods rendered." (Marshall).

III

We have had so many harrowing reports and inspired statements from the partisans of export trade in India about the grave injury to exports.

through a high rupee, that it was considered timely to utter an emphatic protest against the fallacious reasoning and the mistaking of temporary effects for permanent tendencies. I admit that a disturbance of the exchange equilibrium reacts evilly against all trade. The injury to export trade of India comes and has come directly from the uncertainty-bearing element in the exchange problem and not from its progressively higher levels. It is the abrupt jerks, the unknown to-morrow's level, that has impeded the export trade. And it is refreshing to acknowledge that the Babington—Smith Committee recognised the true nature of the issue when they wrote :—

> "If exchange is made stable at a new (higher) level, we believe that the effects (i.e., stimulus to imports and check to exports) are in the main transitory and do not continue beyond the period necessary for wages and other elements of cost to adjust themselves to the new conditions."
>
> (Para 34)

We may illustrate the conditions of rupee exchange by adapting Miss E. C. Van Dorp's figures (published in the *Economic Journal* for December 1919).

With a fixed parity between rupee and sterling as in pre-war times, the rates of exchange can be described by the following diagram:—

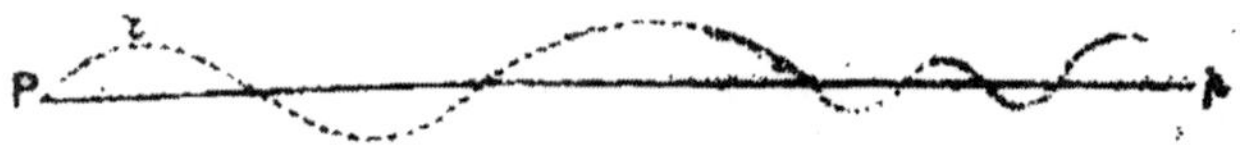

P—P being the parity and r the rate of exchange.

The Rate of exchange (*i.e.* market value of money) always tends towards the parity (*i.e.* the normal value of money) fluctuates about it. P—p. represents the 1s. 4d. norm and the slight variations in the rates for Council drafts and Telegraphic Transfers are shown by the movements of r about the parity line. The deviations away from the line are of a temporary nature and the rate tends to revert back to the parity level.

During war time various causes have influenced the export and import relations. The heavy expenditure by the imperial Government in purchasing stores in India combined with very heavy disbursements on behalf of the military headquarters in Mesopotamia and Africa meant an increase in India's exports which could not at the time be counterbalanced by equivalent imports. The parity was broken and the new conditions reveal this state of affairs.

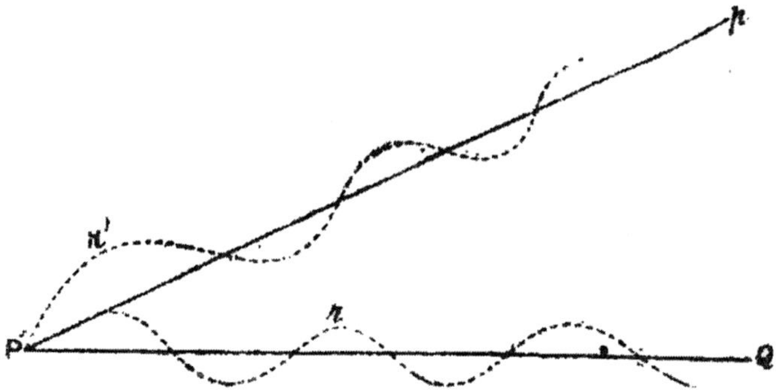

P′—p″ is the new parity level; r′ the rates (P′Q the old parity level). What we have to bear in mind is that the rise in exchange is not a rise above parity, (*i.e.* a market-rate above the normal rate) but a risen parity (*i.e.* a risen normal rate). The rupee parity has risen bodily and we should not mistake a fluctuation in r′ as a fluctuation about the old parity norm of P′Q but accept the new level of P′p″ and measure our fluctuation in rates of exchange by the new standard. We have sound reasons to believe, as we look at the devastated worlds of Europe, the financial bankruptcy of nations great and small, the growing reluctance of the labouring people to remain content with being helots for the leisured few—that high prices and short supplies will be the governing factors of the coming economic life of the people of the world. And the arguments of the Babington-Smith Committee are convincing enough in this respect: that a higher rupee parity has become a real fact for India; that a forced reversion to old rates would introduce economic strains which the social fabric of the Indian commercial world is not strong enough to bear. While this much is granted, it must not be understood that we view with satisfaction or even complacency the way in which the issue has been handled. We will come to it in a moment. Mr. F. H. Lucas of the India Office made a very apt remark in his evidence before the Committee when he said:—

> "I do not think the public in India realise that a high exchange saves them from the worst consequences of the desperate credit inflation here, resulting from the method of war finance pursued in varying degrees of thoroughness by Russia, Germany, Italy, France and Great Britain. To call for a low exchange, *sans phrase*, is ready for India to assume voluntarily a greater share of the burden of the war than she can in fact support because of her masses on the very border of subsistence."
>
> Q. 4461.

It is a very pertinent objection that the exchange method is a very questionable method of reducing prices, i.e. of correcting the maladjustments that may have been produced by quite independen causes. The objection is valid so far as it goes. A non-currency maladjustment cannot be put right by currency manipulation. But surely no one will dispute the virtue of adapting your currency which is in a disorganised state, to a state of things which you consider beneficial and a manipulation of currency for that purpose and that purpose alone should be above blame.

So far the conclusions we have reached may be summarised as follows :—

1. Stability problem presents two issues—the purchasing power aspect and the exchange aspect. The former issue is real by the problem of good money.

2. Steadiness in the purchasing power of the rupee is of far greater importance than stability of its exchange value.

3. An increased purchasing power of currency in terms of commodities (i.e. fall in prices) combined with increased command over nature is wholly good. Steadiness in the real value of money is the one true criterion of a sound monetary system.

4. Rise in the exchange level of a country does not necessarily produce a worsening effect on exports or give a permanent bounty to imports.

5. A higher exchange parity has become essential for India through worldwide causes and not simply because of the monetary makeshifts adopted from time to time in the country itself.

IV

A balanced analysis of the causes underlying the present exchange troubles would yield good results for future guidance, but it is extremely difficult to proportionately judge all the various tendencies and mark out their complex influence. First. we find silver to be the chief culprit and the Indian Merchants, Bureau sends out the *firman* that the silver policy of the Government of India has been suicidal. Dissatisfaction is expressed with the control at the India Office, the secret influences at work in Whitehall and the dangerous impact of the London money market. There is truth in these allegations and a silver control by the Big Two—for, U. S. A. and British Empire are the two chief producers of the white metal—would mean a return to the old *status quo ante* and involve a recurring breakdown in the event of a crisis. The chief objection to such a procedure is that it hectors the currency measure into dependence on political fortunes. And Sir Robert Giffen's dictum against a "managed currency" becomes relevant.

We might here profitably refer to the great complaint against the Secretary of State's methods of raising the exchange value of the rupee. While on one side the Government of India and Whitehall proclaim the difficulties of maintaining the old parity, chiefly because of the rise in the sterling price of silver, and on this account proclaim an adjusted ratio equivalent to the prevailing gold price of the rupee as bullion, on the other side, we have the high authority of Mr. Dadabhai Merwanji Dalal :— "I contend that the price of silver has been artificially forced to its high level by the exclusion of stocks of Indian silver from the world's markets by means of the continuation of the prohibition of exports of silver, and the raising of the exchange rate". (Minority Report) From another point of view, it is quite relevant to argue that the chief difficulties of the Indian Government were connected with the embargo placed on the free import of gold. Had India been allowed to take gold, the necessities of the Secretary of State to purchase silver would have been *pro tanto* reduced and a withdrawal from the market or even a reduced demand on his part may have kept the gold price of silver low, provided the exchange level of the rupee is not raised. The last proviso is essential, for, it has been contended before the Babington-Smith Committee that although the Secretary of State had made no purchases of silver for a considerable period during 1919, the price of silver showed no signs of coming down. In my opinion the cause of this lay with the other ordinances of the Secretary of State which successively raised the exchange value of the rupee from 1s. 8d. to 2s. 4d. during a bare seven months and gave a reasonable cause for silver interests to think that the Secretary of State's withdrawal was merely a "gesture" and would continue but for a short period.

Then again the influences that work behind the scenes at Whitehall are not at all satisfactory from the Indian point of view. An incidental reference in the evidence of Messrs. Preston and Chalmers who appeared before the Committee as representatives of the Eastern Exchange Bank Association of London—a purely British organisation—is very instructive. In reply to a question by the Chairman about the effect of a rise in the rupee upon the import trade, Mr. Preston replied as follows:—

> "The import trade has been very heavily handicapped in many ways so far as its effect on prices goes. You have had setbacks in India itself. First of all, there were the difficulties with cotton and the rise in the market. In 1916 I think the import markets were fairly glutted. The import markets then in Calcutta, Bombay, and Upcountry were fairly well filled. American cotton was rising fast, and the native was not prepared to renew his orders. Later on there was a still further rise. Then you had difficulties with Lanca-

> shire, you had the troubles in India, until at one period just before the Armistice prices dropped to anything like 20% below the filling-in point in Manchester. We then had the Armistice, and there was a sudden break, and prices went down something like 40 or 50% below replacing values. You have had all that drag on you. There again, one has not had a normal position to deal with, and to allow for that the general tendency has been in regard to the Manchester man who has been up against all these derelict goods with this rise of the rupee that it has been a sort of bonus to him and has enabled him in a great measure to get out of what looked like a very bad bargain." Q. 2861.

My apology for this long quotation lies in the clearly defined explanation given of the course of trade in Lancashire cottons and the opportune character of the exchange rise in rupee-sterling ratio so far as the Lancashire interests were concerned. I will not spoil the argument by any belaboured commentary.

Secondly, we have to reckon with the very big inflation at work in most of the European countries which are our customers. Inflation has involved, *mutatis mutandis*, a proportionate depreciation of gold. It is apparent, unless of course we repudiate the so called Quantity Theory of Money, that the prices of commodities in general including silver in terms of gold value will go up. Now we have the accident in India of a silver currency artificially tacked on to gold sovereign and a gratuitous government taking upon itself the onerous task of maintaining the arbitrarily fixed parity ratio. This artificial management can be successful only so far as the bullion contents of the coin do not value more than its face representation. The experience of Philippines in the period *1903-06* and of India more recently is an eloquent testimony to the failure of bureaucratic management when silver has gone up in price and the coin has become more valuable as bullion than as an exchange medium. A reading of the currency operations of the Government of India is very illuminating as indicating the desperate efforts of the government to maintain exchange parity and their ultimate failure. An obvious relief is found in inconvertibility and although alarming but definite danger protests against such a measure are voiced by the European as well as the Indian Chambers with a unanimity that was bound to impress our Currency Controllers yet they have all ignored the fact that inconvertibility is in force without saying so. The Government of India resorted to inconvertibility when export and import of precious metals on private account was prohibited. It resorted to a further step in the same direction when the melting of rupees was declared illegal. This action is in parallel with similar measures taken by the Philipine Government in 1906 when the bullion contents of the silver Peso rose higher in value than the fixed par. That a legal prohibition of this nature renders the currency inconvertible, *de facto* if not *de jure* is not universally recognised. Logically we would say that war measures in England amounted to declaring the English note inconvertible; and that it was so, we have for it the high authority of Prof. Cannon who is legitimately credited with being the first to discover this currency issue. He says in his recently published book on "Money":—

> ". . . . . convertibility of the note into coin is deprived of all virtue when laws against melting and exportation of the coin are present and effective. Convertible notes can then be issued without check just like inconvertible notes, and consequently can drag down the value of money below that of the bullion contents of the coin and give rise to the same phenomenon, a rise of general prices including the price of bullion. . ."

Although in India the rupee was practically an inconvertible coin before the war, yet the further legal disabilities imposed made this inconvertible feature more rigid. A direct effect was the tightening, around the trade movements, of the shackles Indian Overseas Commerce already felt in the official control of the currency and exchange operations. The Currency Commissioner in his report for 1917--18 admits that "imports into and export from India (of precious metals) having been prohibited, the Indian bullion market thereby became a watertight compartment and prices in India of silver followed a course which naturally did not necessarily reflect as in the past the tendencies of the market out-side India." The Commissioner no doubt considers the reactions on his own special province and if he did not indicate the far reaching effects of inconvertibility he possibly felt them as falling beyond his jurisdiction. It will be difficult to analyse the influences yet, but one can instance the ludicrous sight and experience we are having of an appreciating exchange combined with rising prices at home.

In a gold exchange system such as India possessed the problem of control turns on the maintenance within a slight range of fluctuation, a fixed parity of exchange. The current coin in the country is a debased coin in the sense that the value of its metallic contents falls short of the face value. Rupee was thus a " standard token coin", if such a phrase be permitted. Limitation of internal circulation was a sufficient safeguard against depreciation but the converse remedy in the event of appreciation is not available. That the Government of India gave up even the semblance of preserving in force the gold exchange system as soon as silver passed the higher limit allowed by the bullion-contents of the rupee is evident from the announcement made in explanation of the policy dictating a higher parity ratio. An official communique declared that the prices at which Councils would be sold would be—

> " those at which silver could be bought by the Secretary of State. It is not to be expected that he should sell rupees at a rate appreciably lower than that at which he can actually buy them, but he intends that considerable latitude shall be employed in the application of this principle so that as far as possible change may be avoided."

Here is a plain avowal of failure of the Gold exchange system and the future currency policy of the Government was to fluctuate with the unashamed jumps of the white metal. And yet there was a " longing lingering look behind," cast at the old system, since a continuity of the mental coma caused by the first breakdown led on our Controllers to continue devising methods and ways to arrest the progress of failure. They did not frankly give up the attempts to restore exchange parity and thereby initiated a wrecking influence on trade. The element of uncertainty-bearing is a far more dangerous factor in trade operations than a high or low price. And thanks to our gov'ners we are still in that amiable mood when morrow takes care of itself—a principle harmless in itself as an outfit for individual life but hopelessly irritating where collective operations are concerned. It is plausible to contend that Indian trade would not have suffered so much as it has done through this uncertainty bearing figure, had the rupee been left severely alone after the first danger alarm and allowed to fluctuate purely according to its bullion value. Such an arrangement would of course not do (particularly in case of a silver coin) as a normal measure; but for the interregnum, *i.e.* till a definite policy is evolved, such a procedure would, it seems, have been less harmful than the desperate efforts that have been made to prolong the death pangs of an artificial institution in currency.

V

Let us now turn to our economic doctors and their prescriptions. Silver is the big Factor and the future of Indian Currency is indissolubly bound up with the future of this fickle and wayward pet. The Bombay Mill Owners' Association lays emphasis on this aspect of our currency. Proposals to stabilise the rupee need to be studied in the light of the future production of the two metals, their visible stocks at present and the transition policy of the various small states now springing up like mushroom growths all over Europe. We notice the Bengal Chamber of Commerce placing the question of stability in the forefront and urging as a first step the lifting up of the present embargo on gold. An able writer in the London "*Times*" draws attention in an acute analysis of the present position to the mutuality between the future of silver and of the Rupee. While the future of silver depends largely on India's future demand for Rupees, the future of the Rupee depends upon the existing available supply of the white metal, on the probable demand for silver in other countries the progressively decreasing production and finally on the effective application of the Pittman Act. These are all homilies on the Silver situation, And Silver production holds a warning finger against its extensive use, The annual production of the white metal which had increased from 165 million ounces (fine) in 1906 to 226 million ounces in 1911 fell to 164 million ounces in 1917 and 180 million in 1918. If we place this fact side by side with the statistics of imports of silver into India (which may fairly give us an idea of future demand if silver continues as our chief standard) we will appreciate the importance of the silver production to India's currency machine. We have also to bear in mind the agreement, with U. S. A. which Lord Reading entered into on behalf of the British Government at the time of the passing of the Pittman Act that, 'save with the consent of the American Government' neither the British nor Indian Government would buy silver at a price exceeding one dollar per fine ounce until the restoration of the whole 200 million fine ounces taken from the dollar-holding has been effected.

SILVER IMPORTS INTO INDIA FROM 1900 TO 1919

YEAR	Net imports of silver into India Ounces (thousands)		Total world production of silver (fine) Ounces (thousands)
1900	18.646		174.000
1901	49.435		173.000
1902	39.005		163.000
1903	42.274		168.000
1904	79.182		164.000
Average for 1900–1904	45.708	i.e. 27% of	168.400

SILVER IMPORTS INTO INDIA FROM 1900 TO 1919—(*Continued*)

YEAR	Net imports of silver into India Ounces (thousands)		Total world production of silver (fine) Ounces (thousands)
1905	74.349		172.000
1906	84.318		165.000
1907	118.199		184.000
1908	97.915		203.000
1909	73.740		212.000
Average for 1905–1909	89.704	i.e. 48% of	187.200
1910	61.015		222.000
1911	54.876		226.000
1912	32.229		224.000
1913	91.077		224.000
1914	71.107		161.000
Average for 1910–1914	62.061	i.e. 29% of	211.400
1915	55.766		180.000
1916	32.932		161.000
1917	92.194		164.000
1918	74.531		180.000
1919	237.029		(not available)

When the current big coin of a country becomes undervalued because of its increased value as bullion, the first solution—and the only effective one if practicable—that suggests itself is a recoinage of the coins of the realm into similar units with reduced fineness or weight. The same proposal has been put forward for India and opinion is almost unanimous in rejecting it. We have seen that a high exchange parity has become almost a necessity for India. A reduced coinage besides increasing the volume of currency would effect a forcible lowering of the level to the old norm and thereby deprive India of the one method to get away from the discredited influences which reckless war finance has introduced in Europe. There is again the inexorable tendency of Gresham Law and in a country of India's tastes and prejudices the stock of silver needed for recoinage will be tremendously heavy. "The fining down of the rupee," said Mr. Graham, an English merchant, "was out of the question. I would just as soon, because milk was scarce, say by Act of Parliament, that it might be adulterated with water, so that it would go further." Q. 2331. The cases of Philipines in 1906 and of Straits Settlements in 1906 and again in 1907 are cited as instances to the point. But they ignore the vastly different conditions prevailing in these two comparatively small countries when recoinage was put into operation. Philipines boasted of a motley of discredited currency of all sorts when the American Government decided on a reform in 1904. The new system was in force for barely a year or so amid strong opposition from local interests when the rise in the price of silver compelled the Philipine Commission to undertake a revision. Recoinage of 1906 was carried out with great difficulty and it succeeded mainly because of the substitution of a uniform and more stable unit in place of a heterogenous mass of counters which were still in large use when recoinage became necessary. Straits Settlement recoinage of 1906 was effected at the time when the exchange value of dollar was still above the bullion value and the stock of dollars in reserve was sufficiently large to satisfy all demand for coins. By 1917 the Malayan had been accustomed to the use of paper and the currency of the country very largely consisted of notes, while most of the dollars were in reserves. India presents a vastly different problem. The current coin is undervalued as coin, rupee is very largely in circulation, the rupee reserves are not extraordinarily strong at the present moment. Recoinage necessity is not so pressing because of a necessary adjustment we need in our exchange level and an attempt to cut away this support would land us in the morass of higher prices, besides affecting adversely the none too strong financial credit of the Government. I will not refer to the saving on Home Charges from a higher exchange, which a debased rupee will not permit; for there is a counter-balancing loss on India's sterling credits abroad. But this is a minor point and should not influence any decisions which a good currency may demand.

The alternative suggestion of the issue of a 2-rupee silver coin of reduced fineness compared with that of the present rupee, would hardly change matters excepting that the tendency for heavier weighted coins to disappear would become stronger and the demands on Government for the new coin will be immense; for without any attempt to recall the rupees the public would have the open incentive to hoarding and melting.

Finally the impracticability of recoinage for such a huge country as India combines with the risk of grave discontent to show that debasement however honestly forced opens up abuses which no modern Government can venture to risk. Mill's strong language contains a historical judgement on the practice of debasement:—"that least covert of all modes of knavery which consists in calling a shilling a pound—the shallow and impudent artifice of lowering the standard" (*Principles*). The proposals for declaring complete or partial inconvertibility are in the same line. The Government of India were at one time in favour of declaring the note convertible at the option of the Government, until the silver crisis passed off, but they discarded this suggestion later on in favour of the Lucas Scheme. The attitude of the Government becomes plain enough when we remember that "no Government involved in a great war is willing to give up so potent an engine for surreptitiously fleecing its subjects as an inconvertible currency whether in its own hands or in that of the Bank which it influences. For political reasons the Restriction Acts (are always)—continued." (Canon).

It has been indicated above in some detail that Indian notes are at present *de facto* inconvertible. That is the first step usually adopted whenever currency shows signs of trouble. The last measure is, in the event of a prolonged crisis, debasement. The Philippine Government resorted to recoinage in a silver appreciation phase in 1906 and reduced the fine silver content of the Peso by 34%. And more recently the Straits Settlements besides issuing paper currency of as low a denomination as 10 cents have recoined their dollars reducing the fineness from 900 to 600. In India the various Chambers and Bureaus have entered strong protests against debasement. But Mr. Madon of Bombay has in an able memorandum pointed out that continuation of the Gold Exchange system if decided upon, logically involves a reduction of the Rupee. Make the silver rupee an absolute token coin—a note printed on metal (not necessarily silver even) of a nominal bullion value and you can then feel safe from the long reach of the high silver level. Depreciation of rupee can be avoided right enough by limiting supply but appreciation can only be averted if the currency is made inconvertible. But would Indian trade desire to trust the bureaucrats further with an increased control over exchange machinery? Inconvertible currency is the cheapest and most economical of methods but would it work? And experience belies any further instalment of trust in Governments so far as currency is concerned.

VI

The movement for a full fledged gold standard in India found its crowning apotheosis in the scheme presented by Mr. Lucas, which ultimately formed the basis of the recommendations of the Babington-Smith Committee. "India should have a free gold currency, old-fashioned, sound money, free coinage of gold in India, free import of gold, a single ratio between the gold and the rupee applicable to its exchange value, its internal circulating value and its mint par". Q. 4002.

Indian economists have always shown a tender liking for a gold standard and this personal taste has become strongly vocal of late. The halting policy of the Government in the matter of introducing gold into circulation before the war came in for a good deal of criticism; but the management of gold imports into India of late has greatly intensified the distrust in the apparent neutrality of the Government in the matter of choice between gold and silver. A definite charge is made that the whole policy of the Government in its various measures of exchange control "was to compel India to take silver in payment of the balances due to her—a policy managed and settled in London, to the interests of the London Market" (Mr. Dalal's Minority Report).

> "Since 1905 it has been the deliberate attempt of those who control our currency policy to prevent gold going to India and into circulation" (Mr. M. Subedar Q. 3502).

These are grave charges and need a good deal of refuting than is forthcoming. During war time there is no doubt at all that the London Market controlled the movements of gold. Gold plays an important part in the internal economy of India. It serves to divert the demand for social purposes from silver, It reduces the claims made for rupee currency. It has been admitted that the embargo placed on the trade of precious metals brought to a head the difficulties of the Government in matter of currency. We find Sir William Meyer complaining that the Gold Import Act because of the low rate offered did not attract enough gold to India; a greater quantity would have allayed the panic and enabled the Government to tide over easily the very anxious moments it had. "In my time as Finance member we were rather emphatic in our representations home as to the inadequacy of the rate but we were told that the Treasury did not consider that a larger rate was proper". (Q. 3323).

We have also the testimony of Sir Lionel Abraham:—" .... there were authorities in this country who thought reasonably enough that the central needs of the Empire ought rather to be considered and that India ought not to put on anything like a premium to attract Gold"

If London blocked the shifting of gold, India office effectively shut it by fixing a low price which did not pay its import. And did not the Government of India itself in its telegram of 14th April 1919 to the Secretary of State express the desire that further supplies of Gold were not wanted by them although all opinion was at one in considering the continuation of the embargo as the recurring cause of the currency troubles?

The big objection put forward against freeing

the gold imports was the anxiety that India will demand an excessive amount of gold and so deplete the London stocks. We may have outlived the mediaeval age, but our ideas of trade in the precious metals seem to be as antique as those which we redicule in our unguarded moments. We may have derided the Mercantilists for controlling the imports and exports of precious metals, for encouraging war chests and for laying an undue stress on the wealth of the country as augmented by imports of Treasure. But we have our modern equivalents of war chests in the bullion reserves of Imperial Banks; we witnessed rigid embargoes on export of precious metals; we have seen an inglorious exhibition of a wild scramble for gold.

We may agree fully with all that Mr. Keynes has to say in favour of gold economy and join with Sir Brien Cokayne, Governor of the Bank of England, in condemning the policy of "wrapping the talents up in a napkin"; yet we can hold at the same time the view that what is good for India is good for London. When such platitudinous aphorisms as that of the Governor's proceed from the perfectly natural desire to preserve his own stock of gold, it is our right to feel a bit suspicious and enquire if there is really anything behind the pronounced policy other than the mere fact of keeping a subject nation in its "proper place"? Mr. F. C.

Harrison, the veteran economist gives a striking illustration of the relative interests of two countries placed in the position which England and India occupy today :-

> "Where a country is an appendage of another more powerful one, the latter usually takes control. In canine language, it wags its own tail, or to adopt a more appropriate metaphor, the big brother takes charge of the little one. This course has certain advantages in the matter of centring financial management and is certainly to the taste of the elder brother. But a real danger exists that the younger goes to the wall and is left to pick up the scraps from his senior's well-furnished table." (Economic Journal, September, 1917)

Mr. Lucas is reported to have said with full responsibility that—"to withhold the right to realise foreign credits in the world's medium of exchange, gold, takes a lot of justifying and that to make this disability special or unique to India can hardly be justified at all." Q. 4459.

And we strongly agree with him in demanding fair play. That India's absorption of gold in the past has not been excessive or in any way disproportionate on the wrong side is made clear from the following table :—

INDIAN GOLD STATISTIC FROM 1864 ONWARDS

(Average for one year).

PERIOD			IMPORTS	EXPORTS	NET IMPORTS
1864-65	to	1868-69	£6,038,000	£314,000	£5,724,000
1869-70	„	1873-74	3,107,000	179,000	2,928,000
1874-75	„	1878-79	1,482,000	888,000	594,000
1879-80	„	1883-84	3,447,000	83,000	2,394,000
1884-85	„	1888-89	2,537,000	239,000	2,298,000
1889-90	„	1893-94	2,936,000	1,374,000	1,562,000
1849-95	„	1898-99	3,404,000	1,894,000	1,510,000
1899-1900	„	1903-04	8,666,000	4,544,000	4,122,000
1904-05	„	1908-09	11,233,000	5,002,000	6,231,000
1909-10	„	1913-14	21,858,000	3,092,000	18,766,000
1914-15			7,100,000	2,000,000	5,100,000
1915-16			3,500,000	4,200,000	700,000
1916-17			8,890,000	70,000	8,820,000
1917-18			19,400,000	2,600,000	16,800,000
1918-19			1,500,000	5,200,000	3,700,000

The net total absorption for these fifty years amounts to £230,645,000 about 11% of the total production of the world. A writer in the *Capital* of 21st August 1919 writes on the significance of these statistics thus :— "Although the absorption during the last quinquennial period is more than three times that during 1864-69, it represents an almost similar percentage of the world's production during these five years. This coincidence is remarkable considering that conditions were quite different . . . . The fact indicates that

India's demand for gold is for the metal itself, rather than for its use as a medium of currency." The war time figures, however, are for a controlled period of abnormal conditions and cannot be taken to represent a free tendency.

The advocates of the gold standard are undeterred by the experience of the gold standard countries during the war--even the woeful fate of the English currency possessing as it did the strongest financial backing, seems not to dishearten them in their demand. Perhaps it is not well known that America surfeited with gold cried halt and showed extreme willingness to grant credits to one and sundry provided that no more gold would come into the country to swell the already blowed-up circulation. Neutral countries have suffered proportionately more because of their comparatively narrow markets. And the superfluous mass of gold thus thrown in, in place of the normal payment by goods, has enormously depressed their local currency, and a problem created which the safest gold standard couldn't avoid. We have the pertinent remarks of a distinguished economist:--

> "Mere payments in gold which was depreciated already in neutral countries, and after the peace will be so to all expectation in a still larger area, put export countries in a position of gilded poverty, of which in due

> course when the superfluous gold will leave them again at an even more depreciated value in payment of imports strongly advanced in price, the gilding will vanish and nothing but poverty will remain."

He says further on:—

> "Nobody will expect gold to take its old place again. The exhausted nations can utilise their enfeebled energies more usefully than by buying back the gold from abroad in exchange for the fruits of their exertion."

These remarks have a close bearing on the Indian Currency future. I shall not be surprised to discover that the prejudice in favour of a gold standard in India springs out of the natural irritation caused by political subjection. Our economic scholars look at the independent countries of the world—their monetary basis is gold, gold that is an international emblem of equality. And amongst the countries that profess to be more modern in currency methods in adopting the economical Gold Exchange Standard they find India, Philippines, Porto Rico and the Straits Settlements—all political dependencies—and Austria, a political imbecile and a financially bankrupt nation. It is but natural to associate a complete gold standard with what a *Times* writer calls "Indian Self-Determination in the financial and economic sphere". The general idea, seems to be that with the adoption of gold as a standard of value stability would come automatically, for gold will maintain its value *per se*—a doctrine as false as it is misleading. Gold is as much a commodity as a winter cabbage; only it doesn't go bad by sultry weather. Universal demand and universal acceptability have been artificially created for gold—a phenomenon one can locally witness by booming up the Sunday dress of the village belle as a standard of value. The barter value of gold, or still better its labour value, fluctuates equally with cabbage and Kings and if we have placed the yellow metal on the pedestal it is but human choice and human convenience. Humanity needs a great deal of disillusioning on this score and no where more than in India notorious for its metallic hoards. The plaint of Ricardo on this point is very apposite:—

> "It is particularly worthy of observation that so deep-rooted is the prejudice which considers coin and bullion as things essentially differing in all their operations from other commodities, that writers greatly enlightened upon the general truths of political economy seldom fail, after having requested their readers to consider

> money and bullion as commodities subject to the same general principles of supply and demand which are unquestionably the foundation on which the whole superstructure of political economy is built, to forget this recommendation themselves, and to argue upon the subject of money and the laws which regulate its export and import as quite distinct and different from those which regulate the export and import of other commodities."

I have no big quarrel with the advocates of the gold standard, certainly a more independant and commendable method than the so called gold exchange system in the modern era where the marks and ideals of nationalities fiercely clash; where groups submerge only to spring up again in newer formations at each other's throat. But I dispute the false psychology behind such pleas. There is nothing inherent in gold by itself that will stabilise the money value. And beyond this if the adoption of the yellow metal as the standard of value would mark the first step in India's self-determination as well as provide a method of gradual transition from the present chaos, one can hardly refuse assent. But it is preferable to consider if there is not any alternate way out—more economical and stable.

VII

Prof. Gilbert Slater of Oxford and lately of Madras has propounded the doctrine of "paper currency on gold basis" as the next legitimate move for India. He has conducted his campaign with a vigour that suggests the discovery of an elixir for the ills of the day. But a thoughtful analysis of his scheme reveals nothing that could involve a permanent solution. Prof. Slater suggests that the rupee be stabilised at 2s. by making £1 currency notes legal tender in India at Rs. 10 and 10s. currency notes at Rs. 5. He has cogently analysed the experience of Indian exporters in the uncertainites of high exchange. The fluctuating rupee makes Indian trade liable to be charged under the Gambling Laws. He has attempted to look out and consider the alternatives and arrives at the conclusion that his own scheme is best of all because "it pools the financial strength of the Empire, and benefits all portions. It means cheaper food and more employment."

We will take up Prof. Slater's scheme in a moment. It is perhaps instructive to note that there is nothing original in the idea. A study of the Philippine currency history for the period 1903-1906 reveals the interesting fact that an exactly similar measure was proposed and effectively put in operation there when the rise in price of silver disintegrated the "*elastic harmony*" of the gold exchange standard. Philippines is a political dependency of United States. U.S.A. money circulated in the island to a certain extent. When difficulties of maintaining the Peso parity grew big, the Government resorted to a more extensive use of United States currency. The position in India is more or less similar, Sovereign is a known and acceptable coin in India. It is now proposed that its equivalent in paper be introduced to ease the particular exchange position. While we are on this subject we would find it interesting to record that the United States Congress passed on June 23rd, 1906, a bill rcommended by the Philippine Government which enacted:—

> "the Treasurer of the Philippine Islands with the approval of the Governor-General, is granted authority to substitute, for any part of the silver Pesos thereafter deposited in the silver certificate reserve, gold coin of the U. S. A. (which was unlimited legal tender in the Philippines at the rate of a dollar for two Pesos) and to redeem the certificates thereafter issued in either silver Pesos or gold coin of the United States at his option . . . . ." (Kemmerer: *Modern Currency Reforms* pp. 357 *et seq.*)

Alongside place the following from the Budget speech of Sir William Meyer (1918)—

> "We have taken powers to enable us instead of ear-marking gold for our Paper Currency Reserve against the issue of notes to hold a portion of the Reserve in British Treasury bills which are the next best thing to gold. . . . ."

We note here the similarity of thought and action and if Prof. Slater now comes forward with a proposal to introduce British currency notes in India he will be logically following the precedents adopted in a similar position a decade earlier.

The first question that strikes one on reading the learned professor's scheme is about the convertibility of the pound and ten shilling notes. The Bradburys are in fact inconvertible notes issued by the Treasury. English banking circles are agitating furiously for a reversion of the currency policy and Mr. Goodenough of Barclays has proposed a bold scheme for placing them on a gold basis. If they are introduced in India, presumably they will be redeemable in this country, at any rate in rupees. This will be burdening the Indian Treasury with a responsibility it has in no way catered for. I am subject to correction on this point for I have not understood Prof. Slater to say that the notes be declared inconvertible in India.

Prof. Slater has wisely added a rider that "there must not be any expansion of the currency note issue in consequenee of the adoption of my proposal." If there is not allowed any expansion of the currency note issue, the introduction of British Bradburys in India would mean an equal curtailment of the Indian currency note issue—a feature not much liked in our Treasury circles, I expect. While at any time after a few years of the introduction of British notes it will be impossible to ascertain their circulation in India, the Indian Treasury will have to adopt some rule of thumb to be prepared to redeem an unknown quantity of these notes.

And if the financial circles in London succeed in giving a gold backing to these notes, will the Bank of England guarantee to provide India with a gold backed note in unlimited quantities?—a possibility that would carry few odds in favour. I have my own fears that with the introduction of Bradburys in India their convertibility into gold will become more remote and although it may ease British exchanges a bit, there will be no permanent shifts effected. No doubt one of the difficulties in the silver situation is the appreciated American dollar and as Prof. Slater has contended, with the British anxiety in case of Indian exchanges removed temporarily, the American exchange will improve.

But we ignore the possibility of a great depreciation which may set in the currencies of both India and England by delaying longer than is necessary the inconvertibility of the Treasury issues. The London *Times* while recommending that the proposal is "well worth close consideration" has entered a definite negative against it: "but it could not be adopted in the present state of our national finances unless accompanied by measures to prevent the effect of widening the mischievous disparity between our currency note issues and the backing of gold reserves".

Further, will Prof. Slater's scheme permanently stabilise the Rupee? I am not sure if it will prove anything more than a very temporary makeshift. If the Government of India could ease the exchange situation by pumping more currency notes into circulation it would have taken steps already to effect that and Sir W. Meyer's statement quoted above provided the necessary method. For an introduction of the already familiar local notes would be more acceptable to the public and easier for the Government than the imposition of a new brand; and the very notes that Prof. Slater would send to India could form the backing of these Indian currency issues by being invested in the purchase of British Treasury bills.

When the learned professor says that his scheme

means "cheaper food and more employment" he is indulging in platitudes that any quack would recommend for his scribe. If stability of the exchange value of the rupee would bring in more work or cheapen food, it is not the merit of his scheme alone. Free importation of gold or the introduction of a full gold standard would also improve the exchange. These are merits which all schemes can claim until worked.

One word more, I am afraid Prof. Slater's psychology has worked a worng way in submitting this scheme. I have made no mention of the prejudices of the Indian public in this respect. Acceptability is the first condition of currency and if Indian public would rather have a distinct gold coin of their own in preference to the gold sovereign it is playing too much on man's gullibility to think that Bradburys would be accepted. Prof. Slater in his overzealous patriotism—or shall we name it Imperialism?—has given but little thought to Indian needs and sought to suggest one of the ways British Exchequer could be relieved of its difficult position. Here is what he says:—

> "If my proposal be adopted . . . . the superficial strength of India . . . . . will come to the aid of the present financial weakness of the United Kingdom. The absorption of only a moderate number of

> currency notes in India will put up their value and speedily bring the American exchange to par and also prepare the way to convertibility of currency notes into gold."

We might well have been spared the cant of "cheaper food and more employment".

The change from a silver to gold basis may no doubt be likened to a movement towards "bringing the Railway gauge on the side branches of the world's Railways into unison with main lines". But may not the effort seem futile if the main line gauges were being discarded in favour of the swifter, more efficient aerial transport? We will build up our standard gold gauge and perhaps by the time we have finished we will be seriously considering the question of rustication in favour of something more progressive and really stable.

VIII

We have left for final consideration the Report of the Currency Committee of 1920. Incidentally we have touched, during our brief survey, some of the points which have a close bearing on the present situation and which formed the subject of recommendation by the Committee. We will not stay to criticise or even refer to the detailed methods but confine our remarks to fundamentals and attempt to arrive at a correct perspective through an analysis of the basic principles at work.

It is difficult to deny an ability of effort and toil to the Babington Commissioners. They have presented to us a masterly summary of war time conditions in the Indian monetary world and the value of the survey is not diminished by the elaborate apologies which they have offered at every stage for the successive emergency measures adopted by the Indian Government. They set out with the superhuman task to devise means to "ensure a stable gold exchange standard" and if they are hoist with their own petard in their painful attempt after the elusive stability, it is not due to want of toil. They wanted stability; they have urged gold linking of the rupee as a preferable measure to being jacks to sterling. But a gold basis becomes very awkward and even dangerous if no reality is given to a free import and export of the yellow metal, and our Tritons did not shirk the task: they have opened the Royal Mint at Bombay to free gold coinage plus a small brassage! And so the redoubtable gold exchange standard was saved. But what is left of it, one can only conjecture.

The recommendations of the Currency Committee may with advantage be grouped under two heads—External policy and Internal faith. We will consider the former in this section for convenience and reserve the latter problem for our third section.

External Policy: Para X of the Committee's Summary of conclusions reads:—

> "The stable relation to be established between the rupee and gold should be at the rate of of ten rupees to one sovereign or in other words, at the rate of one rupee for 11.30016 grains of fine gold both for foreign exchange and internal circulation".

It is necessary to realise the full import of this change. Rupee has hitherto been fixed in its exchange value with respect to pound sterling and pound sterling was the ideal stable currency till the outbreak of hostilities. It no longer holds that premier position; it has been ousted by the Almighty Dollar and, like a fickle maiden, Rupee has changed her clothes-peg and definitely decides for the powerful rival. The jilting is substantial enough for an award of damages against the Rupee and while we have no doubt that Rupee will suffer the immediate evil consequences of her change of heart through a grave injury to her export trade, we are not so sanguine if the jilted lover will be permitted to gather the damages. It is more likely that the Indian trade will favour to be diverted to a dollar basis—an advantage which lasts as long as sterling continues depreciated—but the material weight of this aspect will not be very significant if British houses control the market through merit of their wares and not depend upon favours from the exigencies of currency patch work.

The plain meaning of the new policy is that the exchange value of the rupee will be fixed in gold henceforth at the rate of one rupee to two shillings gold, but it does not necessarily mean that one rupee will equal two shillings sterling. The English currency is practically all paper now and the Bradbury is heavily depreciated—the measure of depreciation being the London-New York cross rate of exchange which to-day (July 21st 1920) stands at about 3.83 dollars to one pound sterling (a discount of 22.3%). This depreciation as reflected in the acquisition rate for 11.30016 grains of fine gold indicates the exchange value of the rupee in sterling, and logically the rupee-sterling exchange should show a premium of 22.3% above the 2s. parity, if our measures were effective. But they have not been so and the Government of India has frankly given up the idea of a link with gold (*vide* their communique issued on 29th of June 1920).

By this new dispensation there is at present achieved no stability in the sterling-rupee exchange but dollar being the representative currency unit of the one free gold market becomes the governing factor of Indian exchange. As the British pound regains its former position, the rupee exchange will move down until at the achievement of the pre-war Anglo-American rate of $4.8666 to £1, rupee will become 2/-in gold as well as in sterling.

The Commission has arrived at this conclusion for *de-sterling* the Rupee after grave thought and consideration and no one will deny the force of advantages which prevailed upon the members to decide for the gold basis. They have very cogently ruled out debasement and inconvertibility—operations the initiations' of which redounds ultimately to the discredit and bankruptcy of the governing powers, even though they may have been forced to resort to them through stress of circumstances.

We must in fairness to the Committee recognise the clear cut terms of reference to them within which action was to lie. They were asked to " make recommendations for ensuring a stable Gold exchange Standard ". Their province was limited to stability of exchange, and their criticisim confined to the disharmonies created through inevitable forces or through official blunders. They were asked to find ways and means to stabilise the Rupee quickly in terms of its foreign valuta and the one ready method was its link-up with Gold.

We may not agree with the Committee Report in their justification of a particular rate but the choice between sterling and gold certainly lay with the latter if we wanted stability of exchange and that quick enough. A " wait and see " policy involved delay and a perpetuation of the grave evils which threatened the course of international trade. The "rising tide" method by which rupee was to go up with silver prices and to " peg " it there when at its high level as soon as silver prices threaten to come down, afforded no relief to trade and involved a speculative premium where odds are all in favour of the gambler. The rude shock to Indian prices and painful adjustment which a forced reduction of rate back to 1s. 4d. would bring, did not give any chances of stability of relationship between the two units. We cannot ignore the war time succession of strains to which the currency system was exposed; and in our zeal for one set of interests we must not overlook the vaster, greater interest which have been permanently disturbed and slowly readjusted to newer conditions. We may grant all the credit asked for the new policy and still enquire: have the Commissioners really secured to us the boon of stability? As we read and grasp the true logic of arguments ably adduced to show the necessity of a quick approach to stable conditions, we cannot help wondering if the Committee were at all influenced by deeper methods in analysis or by a far seeing provision to distinguish between transitory and ultimate effects. The sterling had cut its moorings and was drifting along and yet sterling was gold in those far off days of peace and plenty. What necessary guarantee do we possess that a change from sterling to gold basis will effect the miracle and permanently solve for us the stability question? The Babington Smith Committee candidly confess their limitation. Their scheme for altering the basis of the rupee hypothecates a regime of high prices and short supplies for a long time and they confess the transition will be slow and gradual. "If, however, contrary to expectations, a great and rapid fall in world prices were to take place, a new element of disturbance would be introduced and it would become necessary to consider the problem afresh." (Para 51).

The new catechism in currency teaches Rupee-Dollar exchange stability. It circumscribes its own sphere of effective action to a regime of high prices and gradual change. The panacea offered to us is after all not a cure against all evils hence forth; it would merely serve as a stopgap for the particularly evil winds that threaten the normally placid flow of India's monetary needs. A change in the course or a diversion of the track would necessitate a fresh diagnosis and another prescription.

Further we have admitted that the parity level of India's, exchange units has bodily risen owing to the stress of world finance and world scarcity. "A great problem of rural pauperisation and internal distribution has arisen within India as a corollary to our financial conditions"—a writer in the *Capital* quotes Dr. Mann as to the unfavourable effect of the rise of prices on rural prosperity and distribution of wealth in India. Dr. Mann's conclusion is that these evil effects are hardly to be gainsaid and that the question of the maintenance of low prices by any means is a matter of much more serious consideration on the part of those in authority than has hitherto been realised. While we agree therefore that a higher exchange level has almost become a necessity, we need not necessarily accord assent to the dead level of 2s. (gold), no more, no less, whatever other conditions supervene or other forces disturb the present relative positions. Fixity of exchange has its benefits but within a limit; it may be purchased at too dear a cost.

These and various other considerations give us great doubts as to how far the Babington Smith policy will effect the cure. They have concerned themselves exclusively with stability in exchange and provided for it under a set of conditions that may not last long. They have given hardly any thought directly to the impact of a currency method on purchasing power stability. This is a defect which through neglect and carelessness festers the economic machine and puts out of gear the most perfect mechanism.

One would not like to suggest that a stable exchange is bad, for it is not. Fluctuating exchange makes a gamble of international trade and even speculators despite their vocation prefer dealings in approximate certainties to those in pure wagers. But a stable exchange is not the panacea *par excellence* for our monetary ills ; and we must realise that its usefulness is limited. To the vast millions of users of currency media the thing more important and vital is purchasing power stability and not a mere exchange stability—a dynamic equilibrium in the costs of living and in matters of deferred obligations. I do not deny that there are interrelational effects but I insist that there are more immediate and more vital issues. Stablility of exchange is a minor problem and depends as much upon our wayward methods as on the fickleness of foreign currency policies. But our Governors think otherwise. In reply to Mr. McMorran about the effect of a high rate of exchange, Mr. Gubbay admitted that "it is not with the expectation or desire of affecting internal prices that they (i.e. Government of India) propose a high rate of exchange; but it is an *incidental* advantage or disadvantage that as a consequence of a high rate of exchange, internal prices must be affected . . . . ". Q. 864.

This is frank but nonetheless disconcerting. Attention has been rigidly directed to the exchange difficulty because of the immediate nearness of the trouble, while the real stability problem is always before us—though abnormal events tend to push it to the background. So far as the Committee now reporting has ignored this problem it has lost notice of the most vital factor in reconstruction. What we need is a system rigid enough to withstand violent ebullitions but possessing an elasticity that would provide for adjustments according to the progressing standards of life among the people.

Let us turn to the second big change recommended by this Committee of experts. Security of a stable gold exchange standard formed part of the reference and the plan to alter the sterling basis of the Rupee was in line with the avowed object. But our Commissioners have walked further in "misgivings waylaid". We find in para 67 of the Report:—

> "The branch of the Royal Mint at Bombay should be reopened . . . . The Government of India should announce its readiness to receive gold bullion from the public

> whether refined or not and to issue gold coin in exchange at the rate of one sovereign for 113.0016 grains of fine gold, subject to a small coinage charge."

We feel bewildered when we attempt to fit in this recommendation with the consistency of the gold exchange standard. Originally lauded as effecting a gold economy, we find the adoption of free gold coinage with a big probability of concomitant waste in internal circulation as one of its pillars! Contradiction in principles could not go further. But we need not go far to sound the logic of the mind that penned the two recommendations. Anxious that the "rupee while retaining its present weight and fineness, will remain a token coin" they advocated a change to gold basis and a high exchange level. But to convert this policy into reality other forces had to be reckoned. A consistent supply of rupees cannot be relied upon because of the uncertain vagaries in the production of silver. There is also the legitimate demand of the creditor to be paid in whatever is most acceptable to him at the time. The Committee has come to the rescue of the Indian Government and suggested a free mintage of gold as the best way out, forgetting perhaps for the time being the principle of gold economy on which the Indian system turned. It is the method of least resistance and will not be open to great objection if it were in line with the avowed principle on which India's currency was to be rebuilt. We cannot have the good sides of two antagonisms fitted into a harmonious whole. The Committee, we are afraid, were betrayed, unconsciously, into agreeing to a proposal beneficial so far as it relaxes the strain on supply of media of internal exchange but utterly at variance with the gold economy principle. We do not know how to name the hybrid. Silver coin is a taken standard, while mints are free to gold—a sort of halting bimetallism which will be a novel experience for currency sensationalists. Point is given to this aspect of the problem by the next logical step in the same direction, viz. the recommendation to decontrol gold and silver trade ultimately—a recommendation already put in effect (July 19th 1920).

In this connection another statement calls for explanation. In para XII of their summary of conclusions the Committee state that "Council drafts are primarily sold not far the convenience of trade but to provide for Home charges." This knocks the bottom out of the gold exchange system. Indian currency is a managed currency and its essential method is to cancel trade indebtedness by the greatest economy through the provision of facilities for remitance to and from the country.

Both Sir James (now Lord) Meston and his predecessor Sir W. Meyer laid emphasis in their Budget speeches on the importance of Councils for trade purposes. Now that the Babingtom Committee have opened the Indian mint to gold they would think that the " way will be clear for the settlement of trade balances by means which are independent of the sale of Council drafts." If the Secretary of State can afford to be generous and wishes to earn the blessings of the mercantile magnates he may, at his convenience. grant the boon occasionally. This recommendation is in line with the previous one, i.e. of free gold mintage, but when viewed in relation to the whole system we find that trade loses the facility of cheap transit without gaining the freedom from Government control which free coinage should bring. Perhaps the Committee shrewdly guessed that under a disorganised sterling exchange the demands on the Secretary of State will become very heavy and a way was found to lighten his responsibility.

To sum up, the crux of the external policy propounded by the Babington Smith Committee was stability of exchange. But as we go through the recommendations made to arrive at it, we are forcibly reminded of Professor Nicholson's query which he put while reviewing the Chamberlain Report of 1914 :—

> "...... in all the various changes the dominant force whether in initiation or modification has been the stability of the foreign exchange value of the rupee in relation to gold (e.g. Sterling). Does it follow because the stability of the gold (Sterling) price of rupee has been established for purposes of foreign exchange that therefore it may be taken for granted that all the other functions of good money are fulfilled by the rupee as so managed?"
> —a query that still remains unanswered.

In plain matter of fact language, the first step in the way of giving a sort of a gold standard to India has been taken. The advocates of a pure gold standard rejoice that in "adhering to gold we have set our course by the true and only compass available for the guidance of the ship of exchange". But although we admit that it is not the fault of the compass that heavy gales are blowing, we are forced to recognise the faulty nature of the compass' make when it refuses to operate or gives false bearings under an electrically charged atmosphere. A more fool-proof compass is needed which will brave the storms and sustain the normal flow and direction of the ship.

Exchange stability is more directly an international question than the real stability. Of course it is desirable that international covenants should govern exchange movements so as to avoid violent and sudden changes. But in the absence of such regulation each country attempts to restrict the fluctuations by controlling its own monetary machine. In the same line it is desirable that world price levels should not be subject to periodical jumps and falls, but when good faith is lacking for mutual trust, it is not betraying the international cause if one single country takes steps to get away from the effect of these fluctuations. Such a measure would involve a disturbance of her exchange stability but it would be apparent to every thoughtful reader that exchange stability is but a hand maiden to steady price level and if we can achieve the latter even though at the expense of causing a flutter in our overseas exchange relation, it would be commendable and well worth the risk. Here is what Knut Wicksell has to say in this connection :—

> ". . . . . over and above the regulation of exchanges by discount rates moving in *opposite* directions there might come about by common agreement a general rise or lowering of rates in the *same* direction when needed in order to lower or raise the world's general level of prices properly measured by some improved index method. . . . . . If not, then every land had better

regulate its own level of its exchanges with the rest of the world, which commodious and desirable as it no doubt is, after all must be regarded as a matter of only secondary interest compared with the former". (*Economic Journal*, Dec. 1918).

So it is not parish patriotism if we set out to correct out own currency difficulties and place the other countries amongst "the rest" for the present. When the Swedish Rikesbank refused to accept gold in unlimited quantities at a fixed price and thereby suspended the liberty of the free coinage of gold, it was assailed for having committed a disloyal action in attempting to check the inordinate rise of prices at home which superfluous gold was causing in the country. But Sweden's action was right; its attempt to "cut off its pernicious dependence on the yellow metal", though not very successful, yielded some relief and has paved the way for the adoption of a bolder policy.

To recapitulate, stabilising the rupee in terms of commodities is the real problem; stability of exchange is a minor issue and depends as much upon our wayward methods as on the fickleness of foreign currency policies.

VIII

It is always a sound method in synthesis that

proposes first to analyse the values of the components. We can then confidently proportion out the parts and attempt to build up a new structure. Stability of money values presents similarly a synthetic side. We are told to observe the causes that disturb the equanimity, and analyse their respective spheres before attempting to build a new constitution. Changes in the value of money has always been a favourite theme of monetary writers, but only few have struck the new line of synthesing the experience. India presents a very rich material for study just at the present. We have seen how the exchange problem has forced attention to our currency methods and in our search for easements we have noticed the pitfalls and the hollows that encumber a smooth and easy progress. We have attempted to arrive at a correct perspective of the various schemes placed before us and have found them wanting in several particulars. More prominently we find them but temporary stop gaps. No effort seems to have been made to tackle the real issue. We have also emphasised the need of such an encounter and in a short way indicated the weight and the significance of measures directed towards stabilising the rupee. I repeat that it is incumbent upon us to avoid giving a further lease to a currency system we have found wanting and extremely troublesome in difficult times. It is all the more pertinent therefore to enquire if we cannot find out something more suitable, more elastic and more real.

Rupee is essentially a medium of exchange for goods and services, present or future. Its purchasing power is what Dr. Irving Fisher of Yale calls the "composite basket of goods" it buys. Can we stabilise this "basket of goods" in the sense that same services rendered will buy the same basket? Dr. Fisher has been advocating a tabular standard of value in the form of a "goods-dollar" and he has shown with great force and cogency I believe, that we can work a dollar of fixed purchasing power but varying weight. His plan is, in his own words—

(i) to provide for the calculation of an official index number of prices;

(ii) to adjust correspondingly the official weight of the virtual dollar at which the government shall issue gold certificates to miners or redeem them for jewellers, in other words, to adjust the official price of gold at which the government stands ready to buy or sell at the option of the public.

The idea apparently is to join together in a harmonious whole the sectional work now-a-days done for limited purposes. The chief necessities under the system would be, first, a calculation of index numbers of prices (which is done by every modern government these days); secondly the business of buying and selling gold—a side in which the Government of India have gained considerable experience; thirdly the business of buying and selling exchange; and finally a periodical readjustment of gold pars—the change to be made similar to the alteration of the rupee basis and the recoinage schemes in Philippines and Straits Settlement, with the difference of a variation as its chief feature and advantage.

The pith of Dr. Fisher's scheme is somehow to bring under human control the supply schedule of money. By sorts of compensatory movements in it the temporary fluctuations on the demand side are sought to be nullified and the variations in the prices level checked, i.e. stability of purchasing power ensured for those "cyclical and secular variations" in the prices level which are today the incidents of industrial life. A Government Board of Mint officials will be charged with the duty of selling and buying currency in terms of bullion in such wise as to maintain "a par not with a fixed weight of gold, but with such a weight of gold as should have a fixed purchasing power". The currency of the country will consist, according to Dr. Fisher, of token gold coins; but there seems no reason why a token silver currency or the cheaper paper one should not work the scheme in exactly a similar manner. Indeed Dr. Fisher claims for his scheme the merit of combining the gold exchange standard with the tabular standard. He deprecates the spectacle of India's "clinging to the skirts, as it were, of the gold standard countries and following that erratic standard wherever it may lead them, although it is within her power by exactly the same machinery, to keep her course steady".

Suppose at any one time the par of price level compares to the gold ratio of currency of 11.3 grains of fine gold to a rupee. If the department of statistics now finds that the average price level has risen 1% that would mean a depression of 1 per cent in the purchasing power of currency. To compensate for this depression it is proposed that the "weight of gold bullion which constitutes the virtual rupee would be declared 1 per cent greater, becoming 11.413 grains instead of 11.300, i.e. in other words the Government will lower its price of gold, and so raise the weight of the "gold" rupee one per cent.

Speculation in gold may be avoided by fixing a slight brassage for minting and by so arranging that the shifts in price will not exceed the margin provided by the mint charge at any one time.

By adoption of the Fisher scheme, we implicitly credit the Board of Mint officials with command over a large stock of gold bullion and currency. The cost of financing the scheme would therefore include the additional loss of interest which a heavy stock may entail apart from the existing costs. India has her own blocks of useless gold and credits which she now keeps for the purpose of maintaining exchange, a far less commendable procedure then "investing" the same amount of stock in a better way in order to maintain real stability.

I have attempted a very superficial summary of Dr. Fisher's brilliant analysis and defence of his scheme. It has attracted the serious thought of great economists and received a sympathetic welcome. But no country has yet formed any opinion about giving it a trial and the reason is obvious. The adoption of the plan would be a definite severance from the prevalent system and may mean failure, disintegrating thus the credits and overseas relations with the other countries which continue on the old system. Mutual jealousies and fears account for the coldness and indifference exhibited towards the working side of Fisher's plan.

If we intend to come to grips with the real stability issue India must adopt some such plan as Dr. Fisher's. And I am confident that an earnest and faithful working of the sheme would be found practicable and highly meritorious for India. We have noticed the remarkable increase in the efficiency of our Statistics Department since its present Head, Dr. Findlay Shirras, has taken charge. Not a very long period should find the Department more efficiently equipped and in touch with the most modern methods. Accurate index numbers would then be available as guide. The second proviso in Fisher's plan is the "sanction to the Treasury to change the amount of gold—or silver—which the mint would give or take for a gold certificate and thus increase or diminish the purchasing power of that certificate". The Government of India has gained a large experience of the gold and silver market. It has already adopted the procedure of buying and selling gold in large quantities. And there seems reason enough to judge that an efficient Board could be developed to work with skill and judgement the Fisher plan of varying the price of gold in currency units in accordance with the variation in price level shown by the Department of Statistics.

Behind Dr. Fisher's scheme lies hidden the idea of the ultimate abandonment of the gold standard. He has accepted the fact of the variability of the value of gold and seeks to stabilise purchasing power by varying the gold contents of the currency units in use. Gold coins in actual use would be an embarrasment; but their concentration in the bank vaults will facilitate a successful working. Ultimately gold could be dispensed with altogether when the people are sufficiently well educated in currency principles; and gold as a standard of value will disappear excepting in so far as it could facilitate international settlements. And if some sort of world action be taken on this principle we will succeed in breaking our dependence on one particular commodity for the plenty or scarcity of our enjoyment of the fruits of our labour.

There are supreme difficulties in the way of the adoption of the tabular standard but the gain is worth the trouble of devising ways and means to overcome them. To expect ideal justice in such affairs would be like crying for the moon. Human devices will but partake of human deficiencies. Dr. Fisher claims no divinity of perfection for his plan: "In short the adjustment like all human adjustments takes place by trial and error. There is always a slight deviation, but this is always in process of being corrected."

We have seen during the last quarter of a century a successful working of the Gold Exchange Standard until it broke down under stresses which assailed its very fundamentals and exposed the weakness hidden behind. The facility of the same standard can be applied with equal ease to keeping the "value of a gold coin at some fixed ratio with the value of the silver coin of another country or indeed with the value of any other clearly cognizable commodity or even with a collection of commodities such as appears in the formation of an index number of prices This was proved by the Swedish experience during the war" (Cannan). Indeed we have to recognise after painful experience the truth of Mill's remark "that there cannot be intrinsically a more insignificant thing in the economy of society than money"; that gold and silver do not posses any supernatural pre-eminence over any other commodity; that human convenience has dictated their use as money for so long and that the same security of convenience will discard their use when they become an encumbrance; and that the large destruction and waste following this world war has brought about a state of things when a consideration of the gold economy becomes paramount. India has been on stilts for so long that the worn out joints gave way under greater pressure. It is proposed to manufacture a new pair for her—this time of gold and silver alloyed and to teach her ultimately to hobble along without reference to any other particular pair of crutches. But gold, the commodity of her stilts, will assume a different and difficult role in after-war economy of society, and the question of the dropping of stilts, whether gold or sterling, becomes pertinent for India. That the world's monetary demand for gold is going to increase disproportionately as soon as the nations get out of the terrible mess of war-relics and post-war effects, goes without saying. The rise in the value of gold consequent upon the excessive monetary demands, will involve a sudden break in the high price levels which are today's feature and which no lover of reconstruction can view with equanimity. Prof. Gustav Cassel writes:— "The withdrawal of gold from circulation and the disappearance of all definite standards of gold-cover have in a most serious degree impaired the stability of the value of gold. If gold is to be used henceforth as a monetary standard, it is, therefore, necessary to take special measures for stabilising the value of the metal"; and all such measures, to be effective, must be of an international character.

When for the maintenance of gold standards some sort of a regulation of the world's monetary demand has become essential, it is not too much to enquire if international regulation could not very well be directed towards initiating some such plan as advocated by Dr. Fisher. While one country by itself can adopt the scheme in toto, an international agreement to regulate the world currencies on the basis of the representative country first adopting it would afford much greater chances for proving the real merits of regulating purchasing power in preference to regulating "gold" than the isolated action of one country.

We do not believe in heroic measures in matters of currency reform. The mechanism is so delicate and the issue so very finely adjusted that prophecy in the domain of future effect from a certain impressed cause often belies itself. The idealistic efficiency of a certain method frequently falls short in practice. It is well, therefore, to proceed cautiously and even timidly along new untrodden paths.

But the conditions have become so diseased in a sense that physic prescribed must needs contain a lot of nerve in it to be of any effective help. When we refer to the state of financial credit in most of the European countries and place it side by side with the great destruction and chaos amongst the producing interests of the world we are surprised rather that the things are not worse than what they appear to be.

IX

We have touched on the idealism of the Fisher plan, but the plan is not beyond the range of practical economics. During our brief survey we have incidentally referred to the favourable conditions that are present in India for its introduction. There is the token standard money and the efficient department of statistics. The Government of India may also be credited with a good experience in the matter of buying and selling gold. The adjustment necessary for a practical enforcement of the Fisher plan will not be very great. The chief element of such an adjustment would lie in the education of the mercantile classes and of the large class of debtor-creditor interests in India.

All the same however it must be judiciously admitted that " time is not yet". The risk of isolated action is perhaps the highest danger and international action hardly seems possible unless of course by international action we mean a confrere of High Finance and *La Haute Capitalism.* To adopt the Fisher plan would mean a good deal of altruism in favour of other nations but international jealousies do not yet permit of an officious act of that kind howsoever charitable it may look.

We will have to look for some other *modus operendi* to achieve our purpose. I believe that the ideal behind the Fisher plan is the true ideal. His scheme may be varied but the principle of standardising the monetary yard stick will remain unshaken. And so long as we fall short of a perfect stability of our unit of account, our schemes must necessarily be defective. But there is a difference between relative degrees of efficiency. We will make some suggestions which will mean an approach to the goal aimed at, and which, because they do not at once arrive at it, should not be condemned on that score alone. Further we will have to bear in mind the necessity of an automatic transition to the better and more stable form as soon as conditions favour.

Ricardo's acute financial mind evolved in rudiments the principle of the economy of human effort in matters of currency. He witnessed in his time the worst form of depression that had till then overpowered the London Money Market. And the strong impress of how great energies were thrown away on such an intrinsically insignificant thing as money stirred him to inspired thought. His "Proposals for an economical and secure currency" is the *locus classsicus* for all currency reforms. The Gold Exchange Standard is a half-way house to the full introduction of a "cheap and secure" money. Why Ricardo figures in all currency reforms is explained by the fact that he, before anyone else, recognised the force of basic principles on which a sound currency rests and he alone, ventured to speak out in no ambiguous words of the "bad state of our currency". His ideas have borne fruit after a century though only partially so.

Ricardo suggested the use of a paper currency based not on coin but on gold bars of a certain specified weight and fineness. Convertibility then, as now, meant a change from one form of currency to another. Ricardo would limit this convertibility to one thing, *viz.*, gold bars which possessed a world market. Paper would be the currency for internal purposes and if the amount of such paper were in excess at one particular time, that is, if it showed redundency and so became liable to depreciation, provision was made for the supply to anyone who offered legal tender paper or coin, of gold stamped bars for his consumption use, or for exportation. International indebtedness would be settled by the stamped gold bars which command universal market and are perhaps more suitable as a basis of settlement between the merchants of two countries than either gold coins or blocks of unstandardised gold. The object was to limit the use of gold to the more essential work of international settlement and use a cheaper media of exchange for home transactions.

The plan proposed by Dr. Fisher is an elaborate working up of the Ricardo scheme to modern needs and modern requirements. His idealism is directly derived from Ricardo, and in his acute analysis Dr. Fisher confirms in detail the truth of the currency principle which forms the essential basis of Ricardo's scheme. And if our proposals for Indian methods directly trace their inspiration from Ricardo and Fisher, we may be well satisfied of their soundness.

X

We suggest that our internal currency should remain as it is, consisting of overvalued tokens of silver, nickel and bronze, and of notes; each fully convertible into the other, and the silver rupee and currency notes unlimited legal tender all as they are now by law. The rupee and the paper should be redeemable at the option of the holder in blocks of stamped gold bars or silver bars or in blocks of both metals. The choice of selection between the proportionate size of blocks of silver and of gold to be issued should lie with the Mint office. The bars should be so made as to be of use for export purposes, say, according to the Latin standard weights. We think that various causes, as shown above, have contributed to a rise of Rupee parity bodily; and therefore our initial value of silver rupee in terms of gold should be higher than it was before the war. We may arrive at the conclusion by means of statistical study that 11.30016 grains of fine gold for one rupee roughly approximate to the parity rise above the old norm, a rise of 50%. We should then be prepared in the first instance to redeem all currency into gold and silver bullion at this rate. This proposition holds *prima facie* from a direct observation of exchanges. We mean in other words that there should not be allowed any "specific depreciation", in the words of Prof. Nicholson, of our currency. We have deliberately left the choice for redeemability between the two metals, to the Mint Controller in order to avoid wasteful speculation at the expense of the Government. For instance when there is an excess of demand for gold the Mint authorities can regulate their offer by putting in more silver with every packet of gold that is paid out. All demands for currency will be satisfied by the offer of exchanging coins and notes with blocks of gold and silver tendered. The rate of exchange which will govern such transfer will be fixed from day to day by the Government with the primary purpose of keeping the two reserves of gold and silver in the right proportion. The Mint Controller will offer slightly cheaper terms for silver if his stock of that metal is partially exhausted and wants replenishing. By this wise the internal demand for currency will be satisfied automatically and relative expansion and contraction of currency will take place without any serious exertion or pull at the reserves. For an interchange between bullion and legal tender coin and paper would mean in the one case a comparative filling in of the bullion reserve against an excess issue of currency—a rupee to rupee full cover; and in the converse case a depletion of the bullion stock means a withdrawal of the currency media from circulation against demands for bullion (a case which will occur when the volume of circulation has grown excessive). Such a contracting and expanding power would be on par with the automaticity which formed the chief feature of the free London Market.

But the real problem for good money is, as we have repeatedly insisted, the problem of stability of purchasing power of the unit of account. How shall we achieve it under the scheme we propose? We have suggested the use of gold and silver bullion as commodities to be made available for social demands of the people and for international settlement of indebtednesses. We have also authorised the Mint Controller to vary his rates for the acquisition of the precious metals in order to replenish his stocks. We will adopt a cautionary point in the variation of the rates, as suggested by Dr. Fisher. The actual shift from one rate to another should not exceed a small ratio, which, we propose, should from a sort of mintage charge or seigniorage on the conversion of bullion into coin. Such a charge usually covers the "costs" of minting in a full valued standard and may be levied either by a percentage reduction in the amount of legal tender coin which would, weight for weight, represent the bullion tendered, or this "brassage" may be gathered in by paying out in full amount, but after an interval of time—the interest accrued for the interval would be a practical tribute levied on conversion of bullion into coin. In our system we propose a similar brassage but with a view to avoid speculation. Without this margin of safety it is obvious that when Government wished to raise its rate of acquisition, say by ½%, speculators might anticipate the change and buy the stock of the Mint Controller just to sell it back to him after the change in the rate is announced netting thus a speculator's profit of ½% against hardly any risk at all. To prevent this sort of gamble on a certainty a small mintage charge may be fixed and it be ordained that as a rule no single change of Government rates will exceed this small charge.

We have thus arranged for a variation from day to day of Government rates of acquisition and sale of the precious metals. If an efficient Department of Statistics were persuaded to help in forming accurate judgments about the movements in price level, we can find excuse for a shift in the rates because of a shift in the price level. The index number of prices should guide the buying and selling operation of the Currency Department. By a regular effective action in this direction we can exert influences to moderate and check the forces which disturbed the price level and so bring it back to our old position.

To revert to our first analogy of the stability problem in currency being akin to the similar problem in ships we notice the further resemblance that for a position of stable equilibrium we need an adjustment so that a slight deviation from the original position tends to bring it back to the old level. We need for this a righting lever which exerts the necessary force. In our currency problem the righting lever is provided by the mechanism of the shift of rates of acquisition as the index number of general prices varies.

The first caution to be entered for is against regarding the index numbers as accurate index to our general state of prices. They are but rough approximations and the nature of the economic disturbance which takes place because of the change in the prices of some commodities in one direction may be different from the effects which a price change of some other commodities may bring about. Each man has a special economic problem of his own and the incidence of price changes never means the same thing to two persons. But our index numbers are at present the only approximately accurate approach to measure the effect of the changes in the habits of a "representative" man who is nonetheless real, though nowhere to be found in actual life.

Our directions to the Mint Controller regarding the effect of a change in index numbers on his rates for buying and selling silver will in the first instance be permissive. The Statistical Department will be his first advisor but he may not accept their direction. This permissive clause will enable us to gauge the true direction of forces at work and to wait for a more definite indication. It will also give relief to the Mint Controller if under special circumstances a strict carrying out of the provision to move the rates with index numbers means a strengthening of the adverse forces at work. We will therefore give him latitude to postpone action in this matter. Moreover as the experiment will be a new one, it is necessary to proceed with caution and be wary of false steps. We should note that we are attempting to control price variations so far as monetary effects on the price level are concerned. A gradual fall in the purchasing power of money due to an increased command of Man over material forces is an undiluted good and we must not be understood to attempt to arrest this progress. In fact what is aimed at is, as urged before, a dynamic equilibrium and not "pegging" the prices at a dead level.

The pivot on which the system will turn is the

stock of precious metals which must necessarily be large and will be more or less of the nature of waste instead of an economy in our currency standard. We keep at present large reserves both in India and England and they should form the nucleus of our new stock-in-trade of precious metals. To ensure full convertibility of the note issue we should perhaps allow for a metallic backing of about 60%—(we will discuss the actual figure in our third section). But our various provisions will need large dealings in the trade of precious metals and consequently a well filled stock with perhaps only a slight turnover will be required. We may here observe that this necessity of trade in the two metals is none of our choice; it has been forced on us because of the prevailing superstition about the intrinsic value of gold and silver *per se.* And until this superstition is discarded we cannot very well hope to get away from this necessity. If things were otherwise we would rather act in some such way:— Suppose there has occured an unprecedented failure of cotton crop in India and the consequent disturbance reflects itself in the general index number: the purchasing power of our unit of account will fall. To correct this tendency the true method is not to contract the volume of currency and raise artificially its purchasing power by making it relatively scarce, for it is a nonmonetary disturbance and any currency manipulation will be of little avail. The best course for correcting the maladjustment will be for a constituted authority to purchase cotton from the world market and pump it into circulation in India—that will be correcting at the source, the removal of the actual cause that initiated the disturbance. In the case of credit inflation at work, thereby affecting the general level of prices, we would similarly act at the source and out at the abnormal bank deposits, say, which are at the bottom of such an inflation.

The conduct of trade operations on a gigantic scale during war time—witness the Sugar Commission and the Wheat Commission, the Cotton Board and the Food ministry—although opening up vast abuses, gives us the hint that the only true corrective of price changes is a stand at the particular commodity which is responsible for the mal-adjustment. We have to recognise that index numbers are never accurate enough to reflect the relative price level to an exact degree. For it is not necessary for the price of each commodity to vary in the same proportion and direction as the price of all commodities taken together. Secondly we must not ignore the fact that prices, index number is after all an average deduction and not a direct measure and accordingly defective to that extent. We will perhaps arrive at a full efficiency when allowances could be made in our measure for various side effects; but so far as present conditions go, our index, though a very rough approximation, is the only measure available. The need for retaining large quantities of two particular commodities in a more or less useless form raises wide issues and the correct balancing of the advantages gained against the dead loss and waste is needed to justify a decision one way or the other. But we believe that some such scheme as we have suggested will ultimately lead to the adoption of a cheaper method as education in our conceptions about gold and silver advances and as we come to recognise their commodity nature. We have to pay the bill for such instruction and the cost under the scheme is much less than the wasteful upheaval which financial crises now-a-days create under the present methods. Then again we have the counterbalancing prevision that as we stabilise the organisation and perfect its automatic working we will save up in ordinary costs so much as will give us ample funds to provide for reserves over and above the convertibility reserves we will require. Under the circumstances we do not think that the cost of the scheme will be an insuperable obstacle in the way of its adoption.

A more relevant objection is the scarcity of such stocks and the "scramble for gold" which each country indulges in as soon as clouds threaten on the financial horizon. It was said that India will make an excessive demand on the gold reserves of the world if free gold imports be allowed, and that gold exporting countries will retaliate by placing some unique disability against India getting it and consequently it is argued, we should refrain from provoking this retaliatory attitude even at the cost of disintegrating our own currency mechanism! One witness before the Babington Smith Committee was frank enough to acknowledge that India's demand for gold will primarily be directed against England and it was England's desire to retain all the gold she can, in her own reserves, and hence the impasse of the Gold Import Act and the denial to a creditor nation of the right to barter away its goods against "goods" she liked best. That it was not fair, is admitted; but that it acted prejudicially to India's material interests is hotly denied, for that admission would involve in its bearing an acknowledgment of racial exploitation being at work. But it is forgotten by the imperialist school that trade recognises no charity. India will not continue to send goods and commodities unless she is paid for in the way she likes—it is the right of owner of goods and services to demand payment in the form he likes. It is a different matter which will pay him best, but the ego of a seller is supreme if the demands of the buyer are urgent. We can not very well see how India could be denied what she liked provided the world goes on wishing and wanting its products.

There would be a prime facie case against India if she were to demand an excessive portion of the supply of one particular commodity to the exclusion of the rest (though I cannot see personally any point in this objection either, for then the excessive tea drinking amongst Russians and Britains would be equally objectionable). But that considering her vast population and resources she has not drawn more than 11% of the total gold production during the last 50 years, there seems no force in this ignorant charge against her of being a "Sink" for precious metals.

We will urge therefore the adoption of this scheme originally propounded by Prof. Marshall in a varied form under the name of "Symmetalism", but with no reference to purchasing power stability. There are no insuperable objections in the way of its technical working. There is a probability of effecting sound changes in our currency system so as to enable it to merge into a more perfect and stable mechanism as soon as the ground is prepared. This method is available for one country independently and we have no doubt that the practice of steadying price variations will exert an influence on the world level of prices and thereby encourage the progressive education of the nations at large in true currency principles.

The ancillary problem of exchange stability is a minor issue compared to our chief necessity. I have indicated above that under our scheme gold and silver bars will be available for export purposes in the same way as Ricardo originally suggested. But we intend a continuation of the present exchange facilities by which the actual transhipment of bullion is saved and an economy effected in our foreign transactions. A system of Councils and Reverse drafts on practically the same lines as now in force (with modifications as urged in the following Chapter) will be in harmony with our scheme. I have advocated, under the section headed Gold Standard Reserve, that a homogeneous system of banking led by the institution of a great State Bank is a supreme necessity for India. I have also urged that the custody of our present gold standard reserve should be given to this bank and the Reserve located in the five chief centres of Indian trade, viz. Calcutta, Bombay, London, New York and Yokohama. There is no fixed rule about it. If Indian trade develops on a scale large enough to need an agency for exchange-control, say at Moscow, the Common Wealth Bank of India would open a foreign portfolio in that city and transfer part of the Reserve there to be of use in regulating and facilitating trade operations. The eminent Dutch economist C. A. Verrijin Stuart writing in August 1918 advocates a currency system like the Gold Exchange Standard for the war exhausted nations of Europe. He urges during the course of his statement the transference from gold to Banks, its function of restoring equilibrium of exchange which it does by actual shiftings or threats of same. He would institute a clause in the Bank Charters that "they should keep at all times a foreign portfolio to an amount bearing a certain proportion to its directly claimable debt and secondly it should be made statutory for the bank that with fall of exchange beyond a certain limit it should take measures so as to make it rise again above that limit within a short period, say, eight days". In case of appreciation of a country's exchange Dr. Stuart does not feel called upon to direct the Bank to stop the progress since the "depreciation of the foreign valuta" is not an internal affair; but all the same Dr. Stuart expects that mutual obligations will be entered into between various countries to effect a consistent parity of exchange.

The cardinal feature of the Gold Exchange Standard—the commodious facility for interchange of local into international currency and vice versa without any shipment of the "money commodity" or of credits from one place to another, will fit in a harmonious manner with our scheme for internal circulation. But as has been repeated often during the course of above statement the chief problem is internal and the chief issue purchasing power parity.

We have seen that our scheme allows for a full elastic working of the three drains which lead from the central mechanism and act both ways, if automatically controlled, in filling in or draining out the central reservoir of our Money receptacle. First, the drain of internal circulation with its seasonal demands and tight markets, will be permitted a smooth course under our scheme. If a business phase needs a larger amount of circulation, it will be because demand for goods and commodities, both foreign and home, has become insistent; or as in particular crops of India, seasonal variations occur at particular periods when a larger amount of currency is needed for financing the harvests. The increase of circulation will be effected partly by tender of gold and silver to our Mint Controller in exchange for currency, and partly by the creation of bank credits. The note issue will be under a self-acting rule and will be able to help in the relief by an automatic release of additional notes against a cover of export bills or short dated securities (This aspect is further discussed under our third section, the Elasticity Problem).

Secondly, against the foreign drain we have provided the facility of foreign portfolios at the chief foreign trade centres for India. Dealings in cover to the full amount will be possible and a very large convenience guaranteed to merchants—convenience which shall be free from administrative exigencies. These foreign agencies of the Common Wealth or Federal Bank of India will also be entrusted by the Mint Controller with the purchase and sale of precious metals as occasion demands. This provision necessitates that with the Mint Controller in India should be associated as active advisors two or three representatives of the Bank. And though the Mint Controller will have the sole power to decide on matters of policy, he should not go against the wishes of the Mint Board, on which besides the Bank representatives, seats should be provided for the Director of Statistics and for the head of the Industries and Commerce Department.

Thirdly, we have to count the drain of consumption. The social demands for the precious metals is similar to other demands for commodities but because of the incident of gold and silver acting also as our currency media it behoves the Controller to provide amply and liberally for this drain.

Only by following a very generous policy in this direction can we hope to enable the people of the country to discard this superstition of gold.

Finally, we have provided for adjustment controls for steadying our price variations the one and only aim towards which we proposed to direct our constructive analysis and which we believe we have succeeded in part to build up. Our schemes and methods cannot work in full harmony with this our supreme object until and unless a ready response is available in the shape of a true comprehension of the nature of Money, its relation to the particular counters in use and its significance in the economy of life—not until people come to believe in the truth of Ricardo's remarks made a full century back :—

> "The introduction of the precious metals for the purpose of money may with truth be considered one of the most important steps towards the improvement of commerce and the arts of civilised life; but it is not less true that with the advancement of knowledge and science, we discover that it would be another improvement to banish them again from the employment to which, during a less enlightened period, they had been so advantageously applied."

India has been credited with having led the way in adopting a cheap and economical currency.

She has given a full quarter of century's trial to the so called Gold Exchange Standard and found it wanting in certain essentials. Would she again be the first to show that a stable system can be arrived at only by relegating the precious metals to their proper place as mere commodites ?

PROBLEM OF THE GOLD STANDARD RESERVE

The problem of the Gold Standard Reserve raises some important issues of policy. It does not involve any deep choice between true and false principles as did our first problem. The question is more an administrative one, of method and design rather than of style. And the problem is peculiar to India in that her currency mechanism was built up of purpose to meet certain special contingencies. The difficulties of silver in the early ninetees led to the closing of her mints to free coinage and rendered her currency the service of the gradual evolution of a method which divorced the value of the metal contained, i.e. the coin from its face value. We consider it a service for with all its handicap the new method secured some definite saving to India. The necessities of particular incidents modified the actual details of working but truly did India "stumble" into the Gold Exchange Standard without being consciously aware of it. The effort has always been to reach the standard of a full valued currency; the technical difficulties of the day postponed action and forced India more and more into the position she occupied before 1913 when the Chamberlain Commission sanctified the method by its generous recognition of the principle of gold economy. Although stage managed to a certain extent the able defence of the system which financial experts put forward on her behalf rested on a true principle. It was the evolution and development of the Ricardian method to save recurring transfer of titles to riches from one party to another as trade swayed one way or the other. With the divorce between the rupee and its metallic value effectively introduced, it became necessary to provide some method of international settlement for what was fixed at 1s. 4d. for Indian traders through an executive fiat although its value in bullion varied from 10d. to 15d. in gold. The rupee could not naturally carry the same destinction in a foreign country where those fiats are not recognised. It became essential therefore to devise a system by which international currency was made available at no loss to the trading interests by this divorce between the coin and the bullion. That a considerable economy was effected in saving the cost of transhipment of gold and silver bullion to the creditor country for the time being is beyond doubt. That an important facility was granted to Indian trade with United Kingdom by the location of the principal funds in London is also beyond dispute. We have fully recognised the value of these services and in the scheme we have suggested towards the concluding portion of the first section we have reserved a place for an efficient control along these lines. We may have condemned the so called gold exchange standard now in force, but its part which refers to international action, has a genuine value and we have proposed its incorporation in our suggested scheme. A discussion therefore on the merits of the problem of the Gold Standard Reserve becomes imperative and we propose to consider its bearings on the currency problem without reference to the merits of the Indian system as it is in practice now-a-days.

The monetary standard in India has not grown along lines expected to be reached or aimed at by its Controllers. While the Fowler Committee of 1898 rejected Mr. A. M. Lindsay's plan for a stable currency yet time has shown how prophetic Lindsay's words were when he said they "must adopt my scheme despite themselves". This feature in the growth of our standard is mainly responsible for the confusions and anomalies that complicate the nature of our exchange difficulties to-day.

The Gold Exchange Standard in its pure form involves the maintenance of a stable exchange ratio. That is, in other words, international currency is always available and to any amount in payment of local currency for export purposes only and *vice versa*. The authority controlling the elaborate machinery to regulate this exchange must keep two reserves in order to be able to meet its responsibility. The one reserve will afford facilities for exchange of local into International Currency and the other for the converse operation, The halting reach of our monetary policy towards the Gold Exchange Standard explains why the very fundamentals such as the keeping of these reserves for exchange purposes only have not yet received a statutory enactment but depend upon administrative fiats from Simla and Whitehall. From 1893-1898 the Government of India's chief aim was to raise the rupee to a gold value of 16d. To secure this end the plan of starving the currency was adopted. Evidently the administrations at the India Office were profound adherents of the quantity theory of money. No fresh rupees were coined during this period and some absolute reduction of the rupee circulation was also contemplated (*vide* Sir David Barbour's "Standard of Value", p. 189).

The Fowler Committee was expressly appointed to help in this rarefication of currency. The Government of India submitted the proposal that a sufficiently large quantity of rupees be withdrawn from circulation and melted down in order to raise the rupee to 16d. But before the Committee reported, the rupee had attained the 16d. par and over £m2. 1/3 (million pounds) in gold had been paid to the Government of India for the purpose of obtaining rupees.

This gold initiated a Gold Reserve "to serve as a bulwark for the maintenance of the Gold Standard." (Fowler Report, Section 40). The Fowler Committee recommended that the profits on the "coinage of rupees should be kept in gold as a special reserve, the ultimate use of which was to serve as a redemption fund for the maintenance of the parity of the rupee at 16d. par." It is unfortunate that the Government of India did not adopt this plain recommendation until adverse times forced their hands. Till 1907-8 the three funds, Gold Reserve, Paper Currency Reserve and the Secretary of State's Balances, overlapped each other and no distinct demarcation of function was made.

The confusion is perpetuated till to-day. Even the Chamberlain Commission did not lay stress on the distinction between the respective functions of the three funds. But it was after the crisis of 1907-8 that the Gold Reserve was agreed to be for the exclusive use for maintaining exchange. It ceased tq be a sort of mere "invested surplus" and quickly became an active redemption fund. The crisis of 1907-8 also altered the composition of the Reserve. It consisted only of gold and sterling securities but the crisis made a heavy and continuous demand for rupees and a special Rupee Reserve of Rm. 60 (Million rupees) was built out of the coinage profits.

It was during the 1907-8 crisis again that the Government adopted in a fuller degree the Gold Exchange Standard by the initiation of the sale of ReverseBills. But the acceptance was halfhearted—there is no statutory obligation and the Chamberlain Commission did not see its way to recommend one, although it advised that the Government should make a "public notification of their intention to sell bills in India and London at the rate of 1s. 329/32d. whenever they are asked to do so, to the full extent of their resources." We will find that the difficulties in exchange have arisen mostly out of the reluctant acceptance by the Government of a policy which circumstances forced on her, "There seems apparent, in the policy pursued". says one writer of distinction, "a disposition to secure tactical advantages at the expense of the strategy necessary to ensure permanent success."

This brief recapitulation of the various steps in-the evolution of the Gold Standard Reserve was necessary in order to arrive at a just appreciation of the difficulties in the position recently created by exchange abnormalities.

The statement before us about the Gold Standard Reserve is dated 30th June 1920:—

		£
1.	Gold in India	*Nil*
2.	Cash at Bank of England ...	1,168
3.	British Government securities (value as on 31st March 1920).	14,528,935
4.	British Government securities since purchased	22,214,874
	TOTAL ...	36,744,977

The classic features for criticism are the amount, composition and location of the Gold Standard Reserve and there seems no reason why we should not avail ourselves of the classic privilege. We will therefore confine our enquiry under three heads.

1. AMOUNT OF THE RESERVE

The Chamberlain Commission did not "think it useful to lay down any hypothetical limit beyond which additions to the Gold Standard Reserve should cease," but they thought £m25 to be insufficient. The purpose of the Reserve is to maintain a stable exchange and so its amount must depend upon the volume of India's foreign trade and the range of fluctuations it is subject to. A growing trade needs a comparatively though not proportionately increasing Reserve; growing trade means in case of India a wider range of fluctuations. The failure of rains coupled with monetary difficulties may create an unprecedented position in India. We need thus an evergrowing Reserve in order to be able to cope with the exchange difficulties which may reasonably be anticipated to arise.

The Babington Smith Committee recognise that the vast upheaval in currency affairs caused by the war has produced abnormal conditions and no safe measure could be applied for fixing any maximum figure for the reserve: they would "advise waiting the return of normal conditions," and in the meantime "when profits again accrue on the coinage of rupees they should be credited in their entirety to the reserve." (para 83). Further the alteration of the exchange parity will introduce some initial strains which will directly affect the Gold Standard Reserve and it is advisable to proceed on conservative lines. India's trade may continue prosperous but you can never indulge in prophecy where such undeterminable factors as monsoon and wars intervene.

The strength of the demands made on the Gold

Standard Reserve by the fluctuations in trade will be made clear from a glance at the appended tables and chart:—

TABLE I

Variations of Metallic Funds at the disposal of the Secretary of State in London (March 31st)

	A		B		C	D
	Gold Standard Reserve		Paper Currency Reserve			× £000
Year	Gold	Cash at short notice	Gold	Silver	Treasury	Total
1906	...	...	1057	...	8430	9487
1907	...	...	1054	...	5600	6654
1908	1131	...	556	...	4600	6287
1909	470	...	225	...	8000	8695
1910	...	3011	375	...	12800	16186
1911	...	1477	757	...	16700	18934
1912	...	1074	855	...	18400	20329
1913	...	1006	915	...	8800	10721
1914	...	25	915	...	8100	9040
1915	...	8	765	...	7900	8673
1916	...	5792	1192	51	7000	14035
1917	...	6001	667	13	5400	12081
1918	...	6000	67	...	10600	16667
1919	...	6016	12	...	14700	20728

TABLE II

	A	B	C	D	E	F	G
							Lacs of Rupees
	Gross Exports	Gross Imports	Net Exports	Net imports of Treasure	Net favourable Balance	Councils Reverse Drafts	Balance Unadjusted
1906–7	17692	10831	6861	3886	2975	4989	-2014
1907–8	17738	13005	4733	3684	1049	1092	„ 43
1908–9	15303	12127	3176	1643	1533	2096	„ 563
1909–10	18788	11706	7082	3113	3969	4102	„ 133
1910–11	20988	12935	8053	3255	4798	3954	+ 844
1911–12	22784	13857	8927	4305	4622	4037	„ 585
1912–13	24609	16100	8509	4415	4094	3849	„ 245
1913–14	24888	18325	6563	2956	3607	4659	-1052
1914–15	18159	13793	4366	1846	3520	-227	+3747
1915–16	19738	13199	6539	1048	5471	2371	„ 3100
1916–17	24515	14962	9553	204	9349	4707	„ 4642
1917–18	24256	15043	9213	2292	6921	5072	„ 1849
1918–19	25388	16903	8485	8	8477	2383	„ 6094
1919–20	32703	20800	11903	1074	10829	5072	„ 5757
1920–21	25635	33551	-7916	-172	-7744	2934	-4810

The horizontal line PQ on the chart represents the period of time divided up into annual fiscal years from 1906-07 onwards. Curve "A" is a graphical representation of column "D" (total metallic reserves at the disposal of the Secretary of State) in Table I. Its lines of reference are the horizontal line and the right hand vertical line which shows divisions into pounds sterling. The datum line PQ is taken to be £m10—as the average balance which is probably an accurate margin of safety.

Curve "B" is a similar representation of column "G" (trade balance unadjusted) of Table II. The horizontal line refers here also to the annual fiscal years but the vertical left hand line is its measure of the ordinate and is divided up into lacs of rupees (the datum line PQ cutting it at the zero point, i.e. when trade is fully adjusted). Curve "C" represents column "E" (net favourable balance of imports including treasure) of Table II. Its measures are the same as those of curve "B"

We must admit that this graphical picture is very incomplete and accordingly our conclusions therefrom must be very guarded indeed. The notion that the Paper Currency Reserve constituted the first line of defence for exchange purposes came to be slowly discredited after 1907-8. That Gold Exchange Standard is the proper fund is clearly recognised by the Chamberlain Committee, but they did not dare to recommend a clear demarcation of functions between the various funds at the disposal of the Government of India. But, as it is, the securities portion of the Paper Currency Reserve shows a constant amount (£m8) till 1912-13 when it was increased by about £m1-1/3. We are therefore safe in concluding that the effect of adverse conditions after the 1907-8 period could be seen from the variations in the metallic funds at the disposal of the Secretary of State. Of course it would have been by far the best and most interesting if definite comparison could be made between these adverse cycles and the ebb and flow of the gold bullion; but want of sufficient statistical data precludes such a course.

We cannot pretend to infer any correlation between the three curves; but there is some sort of superficial resemblance with a slight lag in the "B" curve as compared with the other curves. Certain suggestions arise from their close study and we give them with all the qualifications that are necessary.

(1) The range of fluctuations in Indian trade is one of the supreme factors in determining for future guidance the amount of the Gold Standard Reserve and the length of the range tends to increase with an increase in the total volume of the trade. This is confirmed by the special seasonal nature of Indian crops and their excessive dependence upon monsoonic rains.

(2) The Bengal Chamber of Commerce note of

15th July 1919, suggests that the Reserve should be "sufficiently large to enable the Secretary of State to meet any demands that may be made on him for a period of not less than say two years." The safeguard seems to be ample. It is interesting in this connection to note the suggestoin made by Prof. H. S. Jevons of Allahabad before the Babington Smith Committee. Prof. Jevons agrees with the view that trade balances form the only criterion for fixing the amount of the Reserve. "The main occasion for the Gold Standard Reserve coming into operation appears to be when you have good seasons in India which are suddenly followed be bad seasons". He assumes the extreme case of the exports amounting to only one half of the imports and consequently the normal period of credit being three months all one need provide for is one quarter of the surplus. Therefore, "the total amount of the reserve need not be more than one-eighth of the highest value of imports reached in any previous year". (Q. 4908-12.) The figure of 1/8th is not a precisely calculated fraction but Prof. Jevons thinks "that some proportion of the probable total of imports seems to be the right principle" on which to base the amount of the Reserve. We are in entire agreement with the principle that the Reserve should have a direct relation with trade balances. But any arbitarary fixing of the limits beyond which the Gold Standard Reserye should not accumulate would be in our opinion a mistaken policy. The source of accretion to the fund is the seigniorage profits which provide the recurrent means to add to the fund automatically whenever increased trade calls for an incressed internal currency. There can be no difficulty on that point. Moreover realising well the great thirst of the world for gold or gold credits and its supreme illustration in the scramble for gold which commenced in July 1914, we will be following a shortsighted policy if we do not take steps to ensure greater credits for India in the monetary markets.

(3) The necessity for drawing upon the security portion of the Reserve should be postponed as long as possible. A large portion of the Reserve should therefore be in a liquid form or in a form easily made available in a short period. This feature belongs to our second group to the consideration of which we now proceed.

II. Composition of the Reserve

We have a fund the object of which is to afford facilities for an interchange between international and national currency. The demand for such facilities depends upon the trade balance of the country, which is again responsible for the shiftings in the exchange quotation. It is the function of the Reserve to confine this quotation between narrow limits, i.e., between the gold import and export points. The beautiful mechanism pressed into service is the sale of drafts in London and India at fixed rates whenever asked for. The resources of the Fund must therefore be liquid to a considerable extent. There is generally a minimum which can be arrived at by means of an analysis of trade demands. The Chamberlain Commission recommended that a minimum amount of £15 in gold be accumulated at once and that when the fund exceeds £m30 the amount in gold should not be less than one half. The Bengal Chamber's views is that "a very large portion of the reserve should be held in gold." They remark very truly that "a liquid security is liquid only when it is desired to sell a small quantity and not when it is necessary to dispose of a large block."

And the extent to which the machinery is useful depends exactly upon the power of resilience it possesses, i.e., upon the strain to which it is put by placing liquid resources in the market in the shortest time under stress of unfavourable circumstances. An extra dose of conservatism is therefore needed in fixing the liquid proportion of the Reserve. Again exception is to be taken to the form in which the security portion is held. It consists mainly of Consols, British Treasury and Corporation bonds, and other British and Colonial securities. It seems that an excessive zeal for Imperial patriotism has outflanked the care for security which should be the real aim in the distinction to be made between different holdings in the market. The recommendations of the Babington Smith Committee err on the same side. They believe in "keeping the reserve as liquid as possible by an ample holding of securities with early dates of maturity." They are further of opinion that "the amount of securities with a maturity exceeding three years should not be increased and that the authorities should aim at holding all the invested portion of the reserve in securities issued by Governments within the British Empire (other than the Government of India) and having a fixed date of maturity of not more than 12 months." (Para 84). It seems that our latest Committee in their extra zeal for Imperial connections (quite a natural habit of mind after the immediate termination of a big war), did not give sufficient consideration to the need for rapid liquifaction and independence in respect of realisation, of the funds of the Reserve. We believe that the conclusions of the Chamberlain Commission of 1913-14 were right in their conclusion that "just as London must look to its own resources in a crisis and does not (sic) and cannot count on help from Indian reserves, so India should be in a position to defend its own financial position without undue recourse to the gold reserves of London. . . . . Such reserve should not be dependent on conditions which India cannot control or on resources accumulated by another country to meet its own liabilities." An excess of parish patriotism should not blind us to the fact that we solidify our funds by investing in local and colonial securities and accentuate the difficulties of realisation in the event of a panic in the London market. We should in this connection take note of the fact that gold is no longer the "world's money". The International Stock Exchange securities are already "as good as gold". We have in them a profitable source of investment, plus a sound security easily liquidable when required.

We can construct three successive lines of trenches in defence of our exchange position :—

(1) Gold bullion of sufficient amount to transact usual business and enable the authorities to tide over a minor crisis—say about 35 per cent.

(2) International Stock Exchange Securities—45 per cent.

(3) Long period investment securities—20 per cent.

We have purposely ignored one topic so far—the question of the rupee portion of the Reserve. It is now time to take it up. It will be evident from what has been said above about the mechanism of the Gold Exchange Standard that the change of national currency into an international one is as important as the converse operation. It is a necessary postulate therefore that the system of so-called Reverse Councils be made a permanent feature. And, in order to support them, a sufficiently large rupee reserve should be built up in the country. Its amount would be necessarily smaller than the gold portion; but it should be laid down as a rule of conduct that the long period investment portion of the Gold Standard Reserve should, at any rate, to half its extent (i.e. 10 per cent. of the total Reserve) be placed in the country itself. We may take up the question of Council drafts at this point Councils are the medium by which the mechanism of the gold exchange standard works. They differ in no way from trade bills in essentials. Against a deposit of sterling or gold in London, one constituted authority will give the equivalent number of rupees in India to the depositor's order—the rate to be fixed by mutual contract. During the war we witnessed difficulties experienced by the Secretary of State's nominees in India and he, therefore, decided (1916) to limit the number of drafts sold, as well as fixed the rates before hand in order to control the rate of exchange. This necessitated a system of Approved List, and secret manipulation, a system which forms a subject of grievance for those who could not break into the charmed circle. That it was a war measure, it could be condoned. But in a real effective system of gold economy in matters of international settlement, an active, free, unlimited list is essential. Open tender at competitive rates for an unlimited amount would be the best criterion of trade conditions—a barometer to guide our measures of control for stabilising exchange, and an indication of how far we succeed.

It is a matter of regret and of perplexity that the Babington Smith recommendations take the view that "there is no obligation to sell drafts to meet all trade demands" (Para 61). There is no historical obligation; there is no legal duty; but the essence of the gold exchange standard is not to respond to the needs of the Secretary of State alone but to harmonise with all trade demands awaiting settlement. If that is denied, the system is a sham one and belongs to the category of official impositions, which must be so because they are ordered so. It is on this count that we charge the Babington Report with a contradiction in principles—they would secure stability of exchange standard but would dony the means by which alone it could be effected.

In our scheme of reconstruction, Councils and

Reverse drafts play an important part as representing the cheapest means of international settlement. Council drafts may have originated from the fact of the Government of India acting like an absentee who chose to spend some of his money in England. But their true function is to provide trade with an alternative method of payment. Why gold goes from one country to another in payment for a surplus import is due to the fact of gold being the cheapest commodity you can settle your accounts with. "Council bills have to be sold for a price not higher than the cost of buying in England and sending to India iron or cotton goods or silver, whichever may happen to be the most profitable business." (Marshall). Same holds for the converse operation of Reverse drafts and their unlimited supply whenever a trade demand occurs is essential for the security of our system. We should note that we offer two alternatives for effecting foreign settlement—Councils and Reverse drafts, and exportable bars of gold and silver. Whichever would pay trade would be resorted to and the aim of our Mint Board would be to equalise the two rates in order to minimise demands on itself and direct the settlement by the more convenient and easier route of Council Transfers.

To conclude, the mechanism of free Councils forms an essential feature of our scheme. The funds required to meet them will consist of gold and silver bullion, International securities and a small proportion of long-dated stock.

We touched at the close of para I upon the increased credit an extra large Reserve would enable India to obtain in monetary circles. This can be most efficiently done through the holding of a sufficiently large interest in the Stock Exchange. And as we believe that International securities would sooner or later displace gold in the economy of the world, we will possess in them an instrument to command greater respect and therefore enhanced credit in the Financial circles. The other steps needed to secure this object are intimately connected with our third group.

III. Location of the Reserve

We now come to a difficult and contentious topic. The question of the location of the Gold Standard Reserve has exercised the minds of many thoughtful students of Indian currency and it is a curious feature that while most of the European writers (with few distinguished exceptions) conclude London to be the most suitable place, they have failed to convince anyone amongst the Indian economic or commercial circles. It is not very difficult to find the reason. The relation of a debtor country to her creditor nation is practically one of dependence and in case of India over-emphasis is laid on this feature on account of her political subjection. Also there is perhaps some truth in the remark made by Mr. H. Parker Willis of tbe Federal Reserve Board, U. S. A., that—

> "The Gold Exchange Standard system is available only for dependent countries. In short, it is not a monetary system but a connecting link between an isolated market and the broader market to which it looks for support."—*Quarterly Journal of Economics*, May, 1917,—

an opinion with which Prof. J. S. Nicholson is entirely in agreement. This relation of financial dependence is peculiarly irritating to the intellectual class in India which is, at the same time, ultra sensitive where national interests are concerned. Influences foreign to purely monetary discussion are thus brought in and sentiment blocks the way to a rational judgment.

The subject is of deeper import than what the Chamberlain Commission evidently thought about it. We also note with regret that the Bengal Chamber of Commerce too has not entered into a deeper analysis of the problem and has almost feebly concurred with the Chamberlain Commission's recommendations. It will not be inexpedient, we hope, to revise these judgments in the light of the criticism made above. The most systematic and thorough defence extant of London as the place for the Reserve is to be found in Lindsay's evidence before 1898 Committee. Let us take his seven points one by one.

(1) "London is the centre for the settlement of international indebtedness and India's chief customer is the United Kingdom." There is a good deal of truth in this argument as will be evident from the appended tables. The year immediately preceding the war is taken as the normal type and relative position shown with the year 1919–20.

IMPORTS

COUNTRY	1913-14 Total: 18325 lacs–100		1919–20 Total: 20800–100		Variation in value from 1913–14 to 1919–20
	Value in lacs	Percentage proportion	Value in lacs	Percentage proportion of total	
Europe ..	14710	80.0	11243	54.1	– 32 %
United Kingdom ..	11758	64.1	10492	50.4	" 21 "
Germany ..	1267	6.9	4	...	...
France ..	269	1.4	178	0.8	" 43 "
Belgium ..	428	2.3	70	0.3	" 87 "
Africa ..	369	2.0	348	1.7	" 15 "
America ..	480	2.6	2534	12.2	+ 370 "

IMPORTS—(*Continued*)

COUNTRY	1913–14 Total: 18325 lacs–100 Value in lacs	Percentage proportion of total	1919–20 Total: 20800–100 Value in lacs	Percentage proportion of total	Variation in value from 1913–14 to 1919–20
U. S. A. ..	479	2.6	2528	12.1	+ 368 %
Asia ..	2674	14.6	5855	28.2	„ 93 „
Japan ..	478	2.6	1916	9.2	„ 253 „
Ceylon ..	80	0.4	257	1.2	„ 200 „
China ..	302	1.6	658	3.2	„ 100 „
Java ..	1074	5.8	1965	9.5	„ 64 „
Straits ..	342	1.8	594	2.9	„ 51 „
Australia ..	92	0.5	326	1.5	„ 200 „

EXPORTS

COUNTRY	1913–14 Total: 24888 lacs–100 Value in lacs	Percentage proportion of total	1919–20 Total: 32703–100 Value in lacs	Percentage proportion of total	Rupees Variation in value from 1913–14 to 1919–20
Europe ..	14169	56.9	13245	40.5	– 29 %
United Kingdom ..	5736	23.5	9284	28.3	+ 20 „
Germany ..	2635	10.6	139	0.4	...

EXPORTS—*(Continued)*

COUNTRY	1913–14 Total: 24888 lacs–100 Value in lacs	Percentage proportion of total	1919–20 Total: 32703–100 Value in lacs	Percentage proportion of total	Rupees Variation in value from 1913–14 to 1919–20
France ..	1768	7.0	1570	4.8	– 32 %
Belgium ..	1207	4.8	946	2.9	" 40 "
Africa ..	678	2.7	698	2.1	" 23 "
America ..	2883	11.6	5930	18.1	+ 56 "
U. S. A. ..	2178	8.7	4862	14.8	" 70 "
Asia ..	6191	24.8	10963	33.3	" 35 "
Japan ..	2267	9.1	4823	14.4	" 44 "
Ceylon ..	879	3.5	1187	3.6	+ 3 "
China ..	1330	5.3	2353	7.2	" 36 "
Java ..	193	0.8	224	0.7	– 12 "
Straits ..	655	2.6	924	2.8	+ 8 "
Australia ..	498	2.0	399	1.2	– 40 "

The percentage proportion of Indian trade with United Kingdom was 64.1 and 23.5 respectively for imports and exports for the year 1913-14. The figures changed to 50.4 and 28.3 respectively in 1919-20. The proportion is big and, coupled with India's obligations on account of Home Charges, would seem conclusive. But the balance is not so tremendous and we notice already a change in the returns. America and Japan have progressively increased their trade relations with India as will be apparent from the above tables. We may not consider this feature desirable from the Imperial point of view but facts are there and the monetary standard is not a mechanism to be juggled with for the sake of a shallow and fortuitous doctrine. If America and Japan can afford to provide India with cheap goods of equal quality with British goods, sentiment will not and should not interfere with the free course that trade will take. Business between friends and relatives is always dangerous and the introduction of superficial relationship in business bodes no good to the future of trade between the countries. Still the trade returns, as they are, clearly show that in order to effect economy and efficiency in the settlement of her foreign indebtedness, India, if it is to continue to avail of the Gold Exchange Standard, must keep a stock or reserve in London for exchange purposes. There will be nothing new nor discreditable to Indian national interests in doing this. Other debtor countries like Russia and Austria used to keep a large amount of balance at foreign centres in pre-war days. But exception is to be taken to the character of the Reserve as held at present. The charge against Indian Currency which has not been met is that it is an artificial currency—"managed" was the word used by Giffin. It is the position of the Secretary of State in relation to his powers as regards the fiscal and financial functions that is open to criticism. When one finds the character of disposal of the Reserve made by the Secretary of State, one cannot help believing that there is some foundation in the charge. The way Indian Exchange is made to depend upon the prospects and conditions of London Banking and monetary circles is not only injudicious but seems criminal to the opponents of the system. Although the Chamberlain Commission recommended that India should as far as possible be independent of London as regards its solvency in time of panic, yet they did not weigh fully the consequences that follow from the procedure adopted in regulating the Reserve. India is rendered almost helpless in case London is panic-stricken. The earmarking of gold in the vaults of the Bank of England hardly sustains the belief that in time of storm and panic, it will be utilised only to maintain India's credit. While discounting to a great extent the exaggerated denunciations of the present policy, we cannot help believing that the charge is true to some extent. The course we would advise will, we hope, materially alter the circumstances.

In view of the increasing trade relations of India with America and Japan and more so in consideration of the close inter-dependability of foreign trade to-day, we will suggest that New York, Yokohama, London, Calcutta and Bombay be the five chief centres for the location of the Gold Standard Reserve. We cannot ignore the fact that the amount of the Reserve depends upon the seigniorage profits which again are the result of mintage operations. Minting, it is agreed, must always be the monopoly of the State. So we cannot dissever the connection and the interest that Government will have in the Reserve Fund. But the difficulty can be solved if a Central State Bank be started along lines laid down by Mr. J. M. Keynes in his annexe to the Chamberlain Report. The State Bank would regulate the exchange through its agencies in the principal centres of the world and the control of the Gold Standard Reserve will pass to its foreign houses. We disagree here with Mr. Keynes who thinks that the custody of the Reserve should not be entrusted to the State Bank, although he advises that the Secretary of State "should use the Bank as his agent for the actual sale in India of sterling drafts on London on the occasions in which the Gold Standard Reserve is brought into play for the purpose for which it exists." But why not go a step further and let the Bank have full discretion in the use of the Reserve? The governance of the Bank will be under the careful supervision of the Government and if the Secretary of State is left with the custody of the Reserve to do as he likes with it, it would in our opinion greatly hamper the useful function of the Bank. We will advise the bolder step of cutting away altogether the official interference with trade, except the supervision of the Bank along general lines indicated by Mr. Keynes.

We will have in the control by the Bank a security that the composition of the Reserve will follow sound and safe lines. The existence of a State Bank like the Bank of France or the Reichsbank—both modelled more or less on the Bank of England—procures the unique combination of sound commercial instinct with a broad national outlook. This will ensure a very sound use of the Reserve if placed in the hands of a panel of experts as the Directorate of the Bank will be. Butterfly politicians at the India Office can guarantee neither a sound policy nor a continuous tradition in this matter which so vitally affects Indian trade and commerce.

We have already suggested that the rupee portion of the Reserve should be re-introduced and it would be a source of greater confidence to the public if measures such as outlined above replace the present haphazard policy. We may quote in this connection Sir James Westland's criticism of Lindsay's scheme:—

> "A Gold Reserve intended to support the introduction and maintenance of a Gold Standard in any country ought to be kept in the country if it is to produce its full effect in the way of establishing its confidence which is almost indispensable to the success of the measure."

Lindsay's answer that it was the "British investor who sends capital out to India that wants confidence" is absurdly narrow and does not require any criticism. Sir David Barbour, the distinguished Anglo-Indian financial expert, was also hostile on the score of the evil effect on Indian Currency "that would result from a panic in London at a time when India's Gold Standard Reserve was largely tied up in a deposit account at the Bank of England."

The Babington Smith Committee have yielded to the Indian "sentiment" on this score and as "the possession of public confidence is an asset of great value", they advise that a portion of the Reserve "should be held in India; but the gold so held should not exceed one half of the total and steps should be taken to ensure that it is not made available to the public except for the purpose of export" (Para 85). We need not look into this shallow criterion of sentiment, for if currency measures were to be guided by sentiment and emotion (which must be strongly vocal and insistent if it is to be effective) a short work would be done of all our elastic harmony and our measures of control for solvency. The criticism as we have said, goes deeper than mere sentiment and rests on the urgency of trade demands. To keep it solely in London. to facilitate thus the English trade alone does not conduce to India buying in the cheapest market available and to that extent India loses in paying more for goods she could have obtained, had proper facilities been given, from another market at a less cost. Sir Stanley Reed in his evidence voiced the correct query when he said:—

> "Who can say where the gold will be wanted, in view of the conditions which exist today? It may be wanted in London, it may be wanted in New York or Japan. It is very difficult definitely to say that the only place where the gold in the Standard Reserve can be wanted is London." Q. 4236.

The remaining six points in Lindsay's defence can be briefly dealt with in the light of the reconstruction scheme proposed above—

(2) "That in difficult times gold can be borrowed easily in London at a short notice"—This is not true of India. But the machinery of holding International Stock Exchange Securities will do away with the necessity of borrowing on behalf of the

Reserve Fund. Such borrowing is necessary only so far as a large amount of Reserve is locked up in long period investments that do not find a ready market.

(3) "That India has to come to London for the purchase of silver." This is irrelevant since Gold Standard Reserve can hardly serve this purpose if it is to be the ideal fund for exchange purposes. The Mint authorities should not be allowed to use this Reserve for their trade operations—either the Paper Currency Reserve or some other fund will have to be resorted to. Moreover New York is displacing London as *the* market for silver.

(4) "Location of Reserve in India would create a monetary crisis under exceptional circumstances; owing to lack of prompt gold—India is now protected by a system of Council Wire Transfers." The facts are quite the reverse. If there is a panic in London it would certainly involve Indian markets. Would gold in London or India help to relieve to a greater degree the strain on the Indian market? There can be no two answers to this question. It is beyond doubt that a panicky London will not permit India to utilise to the fullest extent its Gold Reserves if they are in London. Mr. M. de P. Webb of Karachi when asked before the Babington Committee as to his reasons for a want of confidence in the intangibility of the gold

reserve if kept in England, is reported to have replied as follows :—

> "It would be more difficult to spirit the gold away if it were in India than if it were kept in London . . . . . If gold were kept in London and if in a national emergency it was urgently required, the most natural thing for those in authority to do would be to appropriate it. I should appropriate it myself in such circumstance." Q. 1684.

A system of Council Wire Transfers may be able to save India from contagion if there is a panic in some minor market. But if the storm centre be London itself India will precipitate headlong into it without even an effort. The device of exchange agencies of the Indian State Bank will, we think, stabilise to a great extent the Indian markets and enable India to profit to the fullest extent from her gold holdings.

(5) "The habit of hoarding for which India is notorious will interfere with accumulation of the Reserve." That hoarding of gold is not peculiar to India alone was well illustrated when all the nations commenced the big scramble for gold in July 1914. That hoarding is a human evil that takes the uppor hand of man and society when confidence is low is a truth yet to be learned by many critics. The best way to set about remedying the evil is to

restore confidence and not adopt the policy of "give the dog a bad name and hang it."

(6) "The real object is to prevent the circulation of gold in India." Do so by all means. The location of Reserve in India does not interfere with this policy. When it is understood that the Reserve is meant solely for support of exchange there can be no danger of frittering away gold in local circulation provided the Gold Exchange Standard system is definitely and completely adopted. There will be no facilities afforded for change of local currency into gold unless it be for export purposes.

(7) "That transfer of Gold Reserve to India will deplete the Reserves of the Bank of England. We ought rather to strengthen the central reserve of the Empire." The polemics of the national school would dismiss this statement with a cynical remark. The protest of the Chamberlain Commission against the belief that the Reserve is regarded as being available to supplement the Bank of England's Reserve would hardly sound convincing, particularly when nothing is adduced in its support. Witness the astute Sir Lionel Abraham conceding that so far as it gives the people of India "innocent pleasure at not too great an expense, I do not object; but if it were a question of transferring so great a sum that the interest was important and the disturbance to the *Central Financial Sources of*

the Empire was a great consideration I should say it would be a mistake." Q. 5630 (Babington Smith Committee). We will not enter the polemics on this point and will be satisfied with Sir Roger de Coverley's famous observation "that much could be said on both sides".

We have now completed our sonsideration of the second problem in currency. In the course of our survey we have suggested various measures which would in our opinion lead to greater efficiency and facility in the methods of international settlement. But contiguous to this issue is our third problem of Elasticity which refers to the internal circulation of currency, and so forms the other side in our foreign relations.

ELASTICITY PROBLEM IN CURRENCY

By elasticity in the currency method we mean the automatic virtue of expansion and contraction of the volume of our currency units in circulation. Suppose that an extraneous force is at work demanding a greater volume of currency counters in order to meet the increased demand. Our currency will bear the stamp of elasticity if, when this extraneous force has ceased pulling, the volume of our circulation is automatically reduced and a return to the old level quickly reached, unless the original tendency has left a permanent effect on the mark of our currency material. Elasticity is not of the nature of the currency system; it is a superimposed virtue comparable to the putting round an elastic rubber layer round a highly sensitised cylinder and imparting to it the power of response to demands for increase or a diminution in its girth. That there is a standing grievance in this matter of a small power of resilience of the Indian currency no one fails to admit. But the attention devoted to its solution has not been by any means adequate.

The whole problem of internal circulation covers up a host of minor issues and to choose one sensitive feature for our main consideration and elevate it to the dignity of a central pivot round which the whole problem turns needs some explanation. The volume of circulation at any particular time depends, as we must be aware, on the work that is required of our units of exchange to perform. This "work" is capable of direct measurement and depends, besides other various factors, mainly on the total material resources of a country and the exact position which the banking mechanism occupies in our economy. Elasticity is therefore an algebraically computable function of various factors of which the two most prominent are the total amount of business done and the banking habit amongst the people. In England the Bank Act of 1844 went against the virtue of a provision of elasticity, but the conditions of growth of England's material prosperity rose above this difficulty and the deposit cheque system filled the technical deficiency to a remarkable extent. The extensive use of cheques as currency and the potential power of growth of credit that every deposit in the Bank possesses supplied England, as it became industrially great, with suitable means to respond to the needs of a growing nation in matters of currency.

In India the conditions are vastly different. A country of an inconveniently large size to admit of a rapid concentration at any particular point, she has not with her general poverty and ignorance shown any instinctive development of the banking habit. While the banks are very few and all practically confined to big towns the education of the people in the matter of an economical method in currency has been very tardy and slow. And the method of a free credit expansion has achieved but a limited success. The question naturally arises whether we cannot remedy this state of affairs by a sort of compensatory adjustment in the regulation of the issue of currency itself and not wait upon slow evolution of banking credits.

Perhaps it is not fully recognised that the two alternating spheres of action are mutually interacting and influence considerably mutual development. It is a matter of choice therefore to steer our course by the directive compass of one set of conditions or the other one or by both.

It is of our purpose to refer to maladjustments or deficiencies and this rigid feature in our currency demands a careful study before we can attempt to make a choice.

"Money is money by consent, by convention,

and by no divine right or immutable wealth" say the new Oxford Tractarians. There is always something fiduciary in the value of our coins. Where acceptability is the first condition of currency, a part of the value of our currency units depends upon the confidence which people choose to repose in its virtues. Confidence therefore is one supreme criterion of acceptability and confidence is a *sine qua non* for credit. Banking involves a second degree of confidence—a higher virtue than faith in the value of a coin, which is in the ultimate resort a commodity and bears a commodity price of its own, independent of currency use. Cheques and bank notes come under this second degree and a breath of ill wind suffices to shatter confidence in them and bring down the whole structure in no time. When we challenge the written promise of the party who issues the particular currency the measure of our shaken faith is found in the consequent fluctuation in prices. There is the story of the man who decked his dog with specimens of paper money of various denominations and whipped him in public. "Not worth a continental" has become a proverbial saying; and the plight of the imperialist rouble in Russia of 1918-19 furnishes us with a current illustration. "In the American financial crisis of 1907 there were men in New York whose pockets bulged with cheques and other paper

—all of it as good as metallic money in ordinary times—and who could not buy a dinner with it. There was plenty of food, though none of it could be had in return for their money. Such a case illustrates the essential character of money and the perennial risk of its use."

Credit operations therefore form a very important part of our currency methods. The very delicate basis of complete confidence—a confidence which is reposed voluntarily and depends much on individual caprice and which forms the basis of all credit, requires a very careful nurture. The constant danger to which this part of a country's currency is exposed is a continuous disharmony which is always in the process of being corrected: the snag of too much or too little—is a constant reminder for careful prevision. It has become an indispensable factor in our financial transactions, for it consists in the main of power to obtain fluid capital on the basis of a smaller capital invested, plus personal security. Increasing trade demands an increasing currency if it is to keep a level course. Without credit currency the demand on the use of precious metals would be tremendously heavy and urgent, leading directly to their scarcity value and a consequent rise in purchasing power to an inconvenient degree. The late Sir Edward Holden, a noted banker, expressed the view in his address to Liverpool Bankers' Association in 1907 that the "maximum amount of trade which is possible depended upon the volume of bank loans allowed and that the extent to which loans could be granted depended not upon the demands of trade, nor upon the amount of securities offered, but upon the amount of legal tender reserves controlled by the bank." There is a good deal of truth in this remark, but we can very well exaggerate the statement. Credit is built on the basis of bank deposits which again depend on the amount of legal tender reserves with the banks. The position is that of the famous inverted pyramid: a speck of gold at the bottom of the Apex; resting on it is a wider section of bank deposits and bank loans—our credit operations, which again support the flattened top of the structure, commerce. A too heavy weight or a disproportionate balancing of various factors may at any time lead to disaster and our pyramid topples over with a crash. While therefore credit has become indispensable, its delicacy of work and adjustment needs constant attention and careful supervision.

Extension of credit facilities therefore forms an important part of introducing the element of elasticity in currency. While credit creation rests no doubt on the amount of confidence the party issuing it enjoys, its reactions on the general economic conditions should bear a careful scrutiny before action is decided upon. Credit is a substitute for currency in the ultimate sense and an increase of credit means an increase of currency with its concomitant effect on prices. But it is an ideal method if choice lies between additions to currency proper and increase of credit necessary to meet the trade demands.

It has been stated above that "an extension of credit increases the effective power of demanding and paying for goods". But *all extension of credit* does not effect this purpose. Instruments of credit represent an economy of money and in their effect on prices are like other media of exchange. And so far, any increase in their quantity increases the "power of demanding and paying for goods". But there is one qualification to it pointed out by Cannan that "transfers between banks, and between banks and clearing house do not affect the exchanges of commodities". This qualification is very pertinent to the problem before us. In times of stringency the best method to deal with currency shortage would be to devise a network of banks all over the country, in order to facilitate credit operations. There will be strategic centres in large towns whence relief could be hastened along threatened lines in the shortest time. Mere book transfers between country branches and large banks will relieve to a great extent the tightness of the market. For credit is a state of mind or belief. With the development of confidence in the ability of banks to redeem their liabilities the demand for extension of currency during harvest time will be sufficiently met by such book transfers. In U.S.A. it is the common practice for country banks to borrow regularly from the banks in New York and other reserve cities. The organisation will serve at the same time as an efficient means of drawing out the money "locked up in the interior parts". There are certainly enormous difficulties in the way of building up such an organisation in India, but if we consider the position of the ryots, their helpless dependence upon the local money-lenders and the consequent need of organisations along co-operative lines, we can certainly expect for a sanguinary success in our object, if genuine efforts be made along bold lines. It is a recorded fact that where rural credit banks have granted facilities to the ryot, there has been a tendency on the part of the ousted local Marwari to send his surplus money to the banks. We effect double stroke with a single purpose. The ryot is relieved of his vicious dependence upon the local *Kàyà*; and the man with the riches is taught the secure beneficence of legitimate banking.

We have this peculiar difficulty in India. Agricultural interests predominate; the only *banking habit* the ryot can be credited with is his relations with the local money-lender and his heavy indebtedness. While on the one hand the extension of banking facilities is hampered by poverty and the chronic universality of indebtedness; on the other hand the vicious circle in which the ryot finds himself and his scanty returns leaves him with but little incentive to improve his conditions. Sir Stanley Reed's description of it that "wherever you turn in India you find this paralysis of the credit movement arising out of the inadequacy of the banking system" is a perfectly true description. While no doubt it is an axiomatic truth that the "first essential to a great extension of modern banking is a currency system which inspires the public with absolute confidence" (Dalal: *Minority Report*); it is equally true that a *sound* currency system is not built in a day: it is the gradual evolution of a carefully based system of currency which earns the title of soundness. The quality of soundness is an attribute of time which forms the test. And a well thought-out system of of banking helps currency in attaining to that merit, provided the system is based on recognition of correct principles.

In the currency proper itself there is a wide latitude for the application of elasticity methods. "Indian Currency is internally absolutely inelastic

There is on method whatever by which the volume of currency can be temporarily expanded by some credit device within the country to meet the regularly recurrent seasonal demands of trade". (Keynes: *Indian Currency and Finance*).

An automatic power to expand or contract under a strain, is obtained in other countries by—

1. Discounting of home bills,
2. Borrowings from one bank to another,
3. Issue of notes.

In India two external methods are in practice:—one is to buy Council drafts in London and another is to import sovereigns. Both are inefficient for harvest purposes, for both imply attraction of funds from abroad and that incidentally explains the high rates that prevail in India during the busy seasons. Two methods have been suggested to cure this inelasticity. One is to ask the Government to place the surplus Cash Balances at the disposal of the Market. This is analogous to the borrowings from one Bank to another prevalent in U.S.A. In India, Government is a big banker and should take steps to fulfil its responsibility as such, that is, of giving flexibility to currency. The idea of Government placing its surplus balances for loan has been mooted since a long time. The Government discontinued this practice soon after 1892.

Now these Cash Balances are the most peculiar feature of Indian finance. No where, in no civilised country do we find such a huge accumulation of money, metallic money and paper, in Treasury chest yielding no interest, giving no relief to a hard market. The cycle of Government revenue account falls into four definite periods—the third and the fourth quarters are the period for heavy revenue collections. From October to March we find a steadily increasing growth of cash balances. The rate of growth is heaviest during January-April quarter; it is the time for land revenue collection. It is said that all through this period for Government to keep heavy balances out of circulation is to withdraw them from commercial use. And it is forcibly put by a writer in the *Capital* in this wise:—

> "It is this unwillingness on the part of the Government to allow the use of their balances for trade purposes when the money market is tight that prevents the return of the money from the agricultural parts to trade centres. It is this that acts as a clog on the currency wheel. And it is again this obstacle in circulation that brings about a high price for money."

While the indictment of Government policy contained in these remarks is largely true, the policy of lending to the market in the busy season may not so readily commend itself. Government no doubt is a big banker but whether it should continue or not as such is the first question we have to consider. In our opinion the functions of a Governmental department in matters of revenue and account are limited to administrative measures. When it undertakes the difficult task of banking it is overdoing its work and as a consequence muddles over the business to no small inconvenience. But taking the present position while it is to be welcomed that the Government has decided openly to pursue the policy of placing excess balances with the Presidency Banks, the fact of their promise to come to the aid of the market in periods of stringency may exert a harmful influence —or rather a retarding one—on the growth of banking. But the point is insignificant as compared to the necessity of coming to the relief of the market by some sort of elastic manipulation.

But are cash balances the proper source from which funds could be made available? Mr Keynes thinks not. The figures of the Reserve Treasuries (from which alone relief could be expected) show that "Indian money market cannot expect substantial assistance from this source at the time of the year when it is most needed." It is true that after December the surplus revenue receipts far exceed the demands for expenditure but "between January and April such funds are quickly released and returned to the market through the encashment of the Council Bills." Mr. Keynes suggests instead that loans be made from Paper Currency Reserve during stringency for a period of not more than three months on a suitable security.

The second remedy suggested is the issue of notes *without cover* which are to be called in as soon as slackness sets in the market. This is the method of partial convertibility. The history of inconvertible paper is not a flattering one to the issuing party. So Mr. Conant: "Thus far in monetary experience the only practicable means of doing so (i.e. of regulating stock of paper money automatically to demands of trade) has been found to consist in direct redemption at par in coin". The story of American Confederate Paper, French assignats, and Austrian Note Currency is a standing testimony to the dangers involved. And when once a Government is given the power to issue paper without cover, there is no restraining hand on it. The method will be used to cover up all and every sort of currency difficulty.

These two suggested methods are but lubricants—they may smooth away the friction in the currency wheel under efficient working; they cannot remove the clog. The friction will remain and require constant vigilance. Why not attempt to remove the danger spot by means of a centralised banking system? Recurrence of seasonal demands requires as much as a crisis does the pooling of the reserves of the country. A widely distributed and intercommunicating trench system with large reserve depots in constant touch with the most distant outposts would be a permanent solution of the problem. All other devices would be but temporary makeshifts to ease a particular situation.

But there is a third method available through the operation of the Paper Currency Reserve. We welcome the adoption by the Babinton Smith Committee of a plan which originated with Mr. Howard. They recommend the issue of notes up to five crores over and above the fiduciary limit on the security of commercial bills of exchange (initially of export bills only). This is a move in the proper direction and is on par with the practice of United States (from which place the plan was inspired) where Federal Reserve notes are issued to banks on the security of bills drawn against actual goods which are marketed in due course. When payment is received for the goods, the bills are retired and so also the notes. By this self-acting rule no inflation of the currency can take place.

We might in conclusion refer to the heavy absorption of currency during war time, for the usual reason given for it is the same which indicts India as a sink for precious metals.

The following table shows net absorption of currency :—

LACS OF RUPEES	5 years' average 1909-14.	Year ending March 31 1915	1916	1917	1918	1919
Gold (Sovereigns) ..	10,99	7,48	- 40	1,37	11,64	5,21
Rupee & half-rupees ..	8,78	-6,70	10,40	33,81	27,86	45,02
Subsidiary coins ..	62	- 21	36	97	99	2,78
Currency Notes ..	3,39	-3,43	7,87	18,18	15,48	51,70
TOTAL ..	23,78	-286	18,23	54,33	55,97	104,71

That the demand was urgent both for rupees and notes is clear from the table. While rupee absorption increased by a little more than five times over the 1914 level the absorption of currency notes increased by more than fifteen times! This latter fact is called "a surprise of the war"; but in our judgment these figures combined with the figures of gold absorption by India during the last fifty years (table given in Section I) give the lie direct to the charge of being a *sink*—which charge springs possibly from the desire to deny India the payment of her produce in the form she likes best. A part of the rise is explained by the rise in prices necessitating a greater volume of currency. Prices for export rose by 50% above the level of 1914 while the index for imported goods shows an advance of 168. Mr. Findlay Shirras while commenting on these figures indicates in his recently published book the fact of immobility thereby introduced by restrictions on imports. The ryot was prevented from investing his proceeds in the purchase of piece-goods and other necessities and no other course being open to him he resorted to placing them in a safe corner till better times. The ryot is innocent of the banking habit; banks have so far shied of him. Credit facilities being absent, the only lever that moved down those rupees to centres of trade —currency that went upcountry to finance crops—is the normal sale of the ryots' consumption articles. The sale being restricted, the usual solvent of accumulations upcountry during harvest time was absent and the currency that went stuck there literally. We have here in this experience a confirmation of the urgent necessity we have insisted upon to develop and create banking facilities in India if we desire to get away from the chronic evils of inelasticity of currency.

* * * * * *

We have now completed our survey of the field from three different standpoints—three angles from which we preferred to look at our currency problem. Running all through our discussion was a connecting vital thread and it was necessary for us never to lose sight of the unity of the problem. The organic harmony which we believe forms the essential basis of currency mechanism lies in a recognition of the true nature of "money"—its intrinsic insignificance; but there is an imperative necessity so to make our choice that the individual freaks of the commodity we select for money purpose should not affect our broader relations of economic intercourse. Stability of the purchasing power of our currency unit in terms of commodities in general forms the pulmonary vein of our system and without the security of such stability, the vitality of the system loses its nerve power and our troubles, ending in recurrent appointments of Committees of experts, never cease to worry us. The virtue lies in recognising the vital principle and attempt reconstruciton in that light, howsoever difficult the path may be. That such light is not available to our controllers, that they "have failed to advert to the foreign exchanges"—the real exchange of commodities—is obvious from the muddle we have witnessed. Would they gain a fresh lease of control by "amusing us, ignorant subjects, with fantastic explanations of the perversity of exchanges and chimerical schemes for correcting them?" (Cannan).

APPENDIX A

A Note on the Imperial Bank of India

Brief reference was made during our discussion of the Problem of Gold Standard Reserves to the desirability of a strong and centralised banking institution in India. The issue is not a new one and has formed the subject of acute controversy ever since the memorable proposals of Mr. Dickson, the brilliant Secretary of the Bank of Bengal, in the year 1867, who was the first to put forward a concrete and constructive scheme for a 'great banking establishment for British India'. Now that the principle of a central Bank has gained the approval of scholarship as well as authority all obstacles have been removed for the initiation of practical proposals in this direction. The Imperial Bank of India, which started operations on 27 January 1921, is the first fruit of the new policy. To complete the analysis given in the text it is necessary to sketch what has actually been acheived and how far the new event could be reasonably expected to meet the needs of the situation in an adequate and satisfactory manner.

I. Introductory

Ricardo in his cryptic style defines a banker as "only a money lender until he begins to lend other people's money when he becomes a banker". We do not know if Ricardo meant to convey in these words the idea that money lending was one of the necessary vices of humanity, that a money lender was bad enough and that when he begins to carry on his nefarious work with other people's money he turned worse, to wit a banker. Possibly he was thinking of the greed and sins of High Finance which had plunged Europe into a barbaric conflict and let loose the wild, boorish, self-regarding instincts of Man which found an apotheosis in the South Sea Bubble. Whatever be the truth in Ricardo's remarks we find a reflection of the same attitude in a City man's definition of the banking profession, *viz.*, "My brains and other people's money". These words do not mean an insult to the great profession of modern banking but they put in a nutshell the tremendous trust and consequent responsibility which the average person places in the banker. Risking your own money when you lend it out gives you deep thought but when you lend out other people's money, it should give you a twice deep concern. Banking is a great trust and a still greater responsibility.

The huge big Joint-stock Banks which tower the commercial world to-day connote the existence in human relations of an enlarged instinct of mutual trust. The needs of industry have demanded the creation of business morality and the structure of big industry to-day calls for response of a corresponding nature in the banking sphere. Amalgamations and combinations are the order of the day and the new Imperial Bank marks a stage in the development of the industrial possibilities of India.

The Imperial Bank of India is not a pure and simple amalgamation of the three Presidency Banks, though it is largely that. A new turn has been given to the banking wheel and only time can show how far the move was justified by the events. Without attempting a peep into the future we can, however, at the present moment make a profitable study of the promise that is held out. We shall attempt a brief analysis of the structural and the functional qualities of the Bank and find out, if possible a reasoned basis for our hopes and our fears.

II. STRUCTURE

The Imperial Bank of India Act, 1920, provides for the creation of a Central Board of Governors to which body is entrused "the general superintendence of the affairs and business of the Bank." The Central Board does not replace any of the existing directorates of the Presidency Banks. It is a superimposed body of expert and non-expert opinion set up to give a unity of purpose and a coherence of policy to the at times conflicting regional interests of the three worlds into which the Presidency Banks had hitherto been moving. The Central Board as constituted under the Act consists of sixteen members, to be known as Governors, of which eleven represent the interests of the three amalgamating banks. (We include the two Managing Governors in this list for they will ordinarily be chosen from amongst the officers of the three banks.) The President, Vice-President and Secretary of each local Board have a seat on the Central Board. They are all supposed to be expert persons, specialists in finance and banking. The Governor-General in Council appoints four Governors—not being official—to the Central Board. They presumably represent the non-expert opinion. Commerce and industry, the rate-payer and the citizen find in them a distinct representation of their interests. The Controller of Currency acts as a liaison officer between the specialists and the laymen. He counsels and gives advice and at times holds a warning finger indicative of his power of veto over matters of financial policy and disposal of balances; but he does not vote at the ordinary meetings of the Central Board. He is there more or less in the combined capacity of mentor and a third party advocate watching the brief on behalf of the Government of India. The Secretaries of the three banks, likewise, have no vote: they are to serve, we presume, as explanatory agents for and on behalf of their respective constituents. They explain and cogitate, argue and persuade their fellow Governors; but they do not dictate.

The Local Boards remain as before, representatives of the shareholders of the respective banks. They continue as the active authority for daily conduct of business. No fault seems to have been found with their rule, saving the new ordinance that a book of instructions will be issued to them every quarter to digest and adapt if they so like and if they do not, to worry their financial heads for a way out, at any rate, for three months until the Central Board meets again.

While we cannot definitely assert that the machinery of management of the Imperial Bank is designed after a particular type or model, the first analogy that jumps to our mind is from beyond the Pacific. The Federal Reserve Board of America has attained a phenomenal success in unifying and centralising the banking resources of the United States. Without having even a tithe of the extensive banking facilities which the numerous National and State Banks provided for America's citizen, India resembled that great continent in the complexity of her banking problems. Huge distances provincial and inter-state jealousies, absence of a Discount Market, Government control of note issue based on a rigid, non-elastic system, the extensive flank of Government treasuries all over the country—these features among others were common to both countries. And the way how Americans solved their problem did to a great extent tempt our Controllers to think and devise some sort of a scheme on the same lines, if they could not do one better.

The Federal Reserve system aimed to give a unity of life to a decentralised system; the Indian Imperial Bank Act purposes to harmonise regional and communal jealousies and provide a financial centrum for the growing industries of the land. We find the Indian Central Board framed on the principal of security of the sacrosanct vested interests—there must not be allowed the remotest suspicion of infringement of even a supposed right. The Americans imposed on the other hand an absolute executive control over the banks of their country. The Federal Reserve Board consists of seven members, two of whom are *ex-officio*, being the Secretary of the Treasury and the Comptroller of Currency. The other five members are appointed by the executive head of the Nation, the President, by and with the consent of the Senate. The Comptroller of Currency in U. S. A. has absolute powers of supervision and control over the Federal Reserve Banks as contrasted with his prototype's powers on the Central Board of the Imperial Bank of India. The Federal Reserve Board is an active body meeting regularly and very frequently. It largely directs and supervises in a really efficient manner the banking resources of the country. The official yearly report of the Reserve Board is a document of great interest and instruction to the student. The Indian counterpart does not propose to bother about any very close control: they will meet just once in three months, discuss a few amendments to Bye-Laws, air some grievances and wait for the next quarter to throw up its own local troubles to provide enough agenda for a meeting. We do not wish to be disparaging but in comparison the Indian Central Board seems to have been constituted on a boneless principle. No initiative in policy is possible for it, nor any immediate control to rectify the possible infringements of Central policy by one of the member banks.

It was suggested that we might have copied another American model and embodied in the constitution some sort of a Federal Advisory Council. This latter body in the United States is composed of one nominee each of the several Reserve Banks. It meets four times in the year and though it can call for information and confer direct with the Federal Reserve Board, its functions are purely consultative. We would have thought that in work, not in constitution, the Central Board in India would resemble the Federal Advisory Council. And our doubts lie exactly in the relative invertebracy of the Central Board. The reasoned opinion of Prof. Sprague about the Federal Council is significant:

> "With a scattered membership and holding regular meetings only at long intervals, it is not to be expected that the Council will be in close touch with the Federal Reserve Board, or be in a position to formulate policies and urge them effectively . . . the work of the Council as an organised body seems likely to be of a formal and perfunctory nature."

We feel the same sort of fears as we note the mechanism and working of the Central Board of the Imperial Bank of India. No doubt it is endowed with the managing and executive authority over the Imperial Bank, but in detail the Board works out to be merely a Board of Trustees watching the interests of the respective wards and spheres of the members, and coming together only when in conflict. A constructive line of advance cannot be formulated, nor the enforcement of a well-laid policy closely supervised in practice.

There is another model which provided the Government of India enough instruction for a banking legislation on parallel lines. The German Reichsbank Act modelled after the heart of the bureaucrats could not, however, be followed in strict details, but a few of the precepts learnt therefrom stuck in the memory of the framers of the Imperial Bank of India Act. We note, for instance, that the supreme body in the Reichsbank Act known as the Bank-Kuratorium is entirely nominated by the Emperor meets four times in the year to receive general report and accounts, and watches on behalf of the Imperial Government the strict carrying out of the Reichsbank's financial obligation. The Kuratorium is avowedly a Board of Trustees with no control in the active conduct of the Bank. The next authority in the Reichsbank is the Bank-Directorium to whom is entrusted the supreme management of the bank. This too is a Government Committee and though it meets frequently it is generally guided by the Shareholders' Committee which legally is purely consultative.

How far the legislative department of the Government of India was influenced by the German constitution in framing the Bank Act cannot be accurately determined, but we can notice a distinct effort to model the Boards on the same lines. We know the great difficulties of compromise and accommodation which provincial jealousies warranted; we also realise the strength of the argument that decentralised local administration combined with a unitary policy gives the best results. The prevailing line of advance in the English banking world is towards amalgamation wholesale but with this difference that the smaller banks retain their local management and their directorate with knowledge of local conditions find a seat on the Head Office Board. A similar thought governs the clause in the Imperial Bank of India Act which gives almost completely independent control of Local Boards. But, at the same time, though fully appreciating the virtues of such arrangement and the impediments in the way of close centralisation one cannot help noticing the ineffective character of the Central Board as constituted. It can lay down a policy if the individual Governors possess the energy of initiative but they cannot see it worked. Its powers would show more in the nature of a negative control than in the evolution of a continuous constructive programme of banking development.

III. MECHANISM

In this section we propose to deal with the daily 'bread' of the Bank--the mechanical outfit with which it is launched in the wide monetary stream and which is expected to keep it afloat and bring it safe into the haven of prosperity. Mechanics is rather an ambiguous word for we do not mean by it any thing more than the actual Capital and Reserves and Deposits which form the basis of a Bank's daily transactions; we also presuppose growth in these elements, i.e., elasticity in working. Strictly we will confine ourselves to the initial outfit and Mechanics is hardly the suitable word to describe it save in its elementary sense of support, but in the absence of any other more accurate phraseology this may pass.

Immediately prior to the amalgamation the position indicated the following :—

—	Capital	Reserves	DEPOSITS Govt.	Private	Total	Cash
Bank of Bengal ...	200	210	388	3439	3827	1244
Bank of Bonbay ...	100	125	187	2650	2837	980
Bank of Madras ...	75	45	124	1529	1653	455
TOTAL ...	375	380	699	7618	8317	2679

(In Lakhs of Rupees)

The amalgamated Imperial Bank of India shows an authorised Capital of Rs. 1125 lakhs with one-half paid up and a Reserve of 375 lakhs. Of the increased capital the amalgam contributed 375 lakhs fully paid up. 750 lakhs of new capital has been issued of shares of Rs. 500 each and has been offered in the first instance to the existing shareholders of the Bank of Bengal and Bombay at par and the shareholders of the Bank of Madras at a premium of Rs. 100. A call of Rs. 125 only is made on these new shares. We notice that the new shares not taken by the old share-holders have been offered to the public on the tender system. The adjustments necessary to place all the old shareholders at an equal footing has resulted in a diminution of the Reserves which are expected to stand at the figure of approximately 375 lakhs after the new shares have all been taken up. The position is therefore as follows:—

Authorised Capital	1125	Lakhs of Rupees
Paid up „	562½	„
Reserves „	375	„
Reserve liability	562½	„

Although Mr. Keynes in his valuable Memorandum on the State Bank to the Chamberlain Commission of 1914 discounted all claims for an increase of capital and saw no reason for the fears of the Government of India in respect of a low capitalisation, it seems that the Government persisted in exacting a fuller security in return for the use of its Balances. Perhaps the abnormal expansion of the post war era had also some influence in advising for increased capital. Mr. Findlay Shirras quotes an article from the *Times* of 14 March 1913 as referring to the inadequate capitalisation of the Presidency Banks :—

> "India suffers from a vast amount of infructuous capital which a State Bank would be likely to draw forth in the shape of shares or deposits. . . . . .
>
> Given a state Bank with large capital and plenty of resources the Government could again keep its headquarter balances in bank custody without any apprehension of monetary disturbances in consequence of withdrawals, and, on the other hand, it would be able to depend on the bank to advance money if the needs of the state momentarily required the assistance."

Increase in capital is therefore supposed to serve a double policy: an additional security to the government and a sufficiency of working capital in the daily business of the bank.

The change initiated by the amalgamation of the three Presidency Banks has also influenced the Deposits side of the new Bank. Besides what the additional prestige and strength may bring by directing the accelerated flow of private money into the coffers of the Imperial Bank, the connection with the government treasury has been strengthened and the Bank becomes its sole banker in India. Where ever the Bank will have a branch it will henceforth be able to claim the balances of the place; the reserve treasuries have been abolished and the Bank will "pay, collect, receive and remit money, bullion and securities on behalf of the government". One salutary effect of this provision has been the reduction of the costs of remittance from one place to another in the country, for the Bank now gives facilities to the general public to transfer money at the rates not in excess of those approved by the Controller of Currency. The result has been that the usual charge of 4 annas per cent. has now been reduced to 1 anna per cent. for sums below Rs. 10,000 and to 2 annas per cent. for sums over Rs. 10,000.

The re-arrangement of the capital and reserves of the three Presidency Banks owing to amalgamation has resulted, as stated above in a lowering of the Reserves. The Balance Sheet as it stood on 30th June 1921 shows:—

THE BALANCE SHEET ON 30TH JUNE 1921

Liabilities	Rs.	Assets	Rs.
Subscribed Capital	10.65.73.000	Government Securities	15.17.39.984
		Other Authorised Securities ...	1.35.25.004
Capital paid up	5.47.68.250	Loans	13.96.25.465
Reserve	3.71.21.400	Cash Credits	22.57.13.176
Public Deposits	22.20.00.953	Inland Bills discounted & purchased	13.12.50.438
Other Deposits	70.16.37.999	Foreign Bills discounted and purchased	38.746
Loans against securities per contra.	55.41.463	Bullion	8.386
Sundries	97.71.979	Dead Stock	2.06.01.346
		Sundries	32.17.199
		Balances with other Banks ...	16.52.718
			68.73.72.462
		Cash	34.34.69.578
Total ...	103.08.42.044	Total ...	103.08.42.044

Balance Sheet includes :—

Deposits in London	£ 21.832
Advances in London	„ 382.144
Cash and Balance with other banks ...	„ 99.586

Reserve

Balance on 27–1–1921 (date of amalgamation)	Rs.	345.00.000
Premium on new shares	„	26.21.400
Added from profits ended 30–6–1921	„	10.00.000
Total	Rs.	381.21.400

* * * *

The Government has safeguarded its position which the abolition of the reserve treasuries entailed by providing that the "Governor-General in Council should have power to issue instructions to the Bank in respect of any matter which in his opinion vitally affected his financial policy or the safety of the Government balances". It is in pursuance of this provision that the representative of the Government on the Central Board has been given the power of holding up any policy or move which he considers inimical to the interests of the Government. In return for the services the Bank is given the use of the government funds free of interest—a very valuable concession when we notice that the government reserves no right to share in the profits: a procedure usually adopted in all State Banks. This is only a tentative arrangement till the Bank finds its way during the first few years of its progress and is subject to revision later. It is considered a sufficient recompense if the Bank opens at least 100 branches during the first five years. The controversy whether a State Bank should retain all private capital or share the capital between the public and the state or be wholly state-owned cannot be definitely settled without reference to the particular circumstances of the country. In India the Government has chosen to stand aside and refuse all participation both in the capital and the profits for the time being. The problem is complicated here because of the inter-racial jealousies between the British and the Indian interests and no definite lesson could be learned from the experiences of other countries possessing State Banks like Germany or Belgium and France. As a general guide the words of Prof. Lexis (as quoted by Mr. Keynes) are instructive: ". . . . a bank of issue (which the Imperial Bank of India is not yet) even when entirely managed by the State has a sort of independence with private capital . . . an independence which protects it against interference with the vital conditions of its existance. . . never forget that a great private capital is in its charge. The Central Committee of the Reichsbank has undoubtedly only a very moderate authority, but its influence, nevertheless, is far greater than that of an advisory board of a State railroad company, because it represents the owners of the bank capital."

The mangement of the Public Debt was already in the hands of the Bank of Bengal and the Imperial Bank retains the work under the provision that the Bank "shall under and subject to the orders of the Governor General in Council or the Controller of Currency use its best endeavours to decentralise the administration of the public debt and to distribute the same amongst its various local head offices and branches". As remuneration the Bank is allowed a commission at the rate of Rs. 2000 per crore per annum on the "amount of the public debt on the books of the Public Debt Offices", excluding (1) the amounts of loans discharged outstanding after one year from the date of a notice of discharge; (2) the amount of the currency investment; (3) the amount of stock certificates for Rs. 50,000 and upwards held by the Controller of the Currency: (4) the amount of stocks and notes outstanding in the London Register. The Bank is further allowed a fixed sum of Rs. 2,000 a year on account of the stock certificates mentioned in (3) above. If the Bank manages the debt work for a local Government the commission rate is Rs. 3,000 per crore instead. The end in view of this arrangement is to secure in the words of Mr. Howard, ex-Controller of Currency and Secretary Finance Department, that "a considerable portion of the work connected with small holdings of securities shall be conducted in the districts in which these are held, and that in course of time as the new bank establishes branches in every district the majority of up-country holders will be enabled to put through at their district headquarters all business connected with their securities."

IV. FUNCTION

Before we enter into a detailed survey of the particular virtues we may expect to flow from the incorporation of the three Presidency Banks into the Imperial Bank of India, it will be helpful if we disabuse our minds regarding two very current notions. First, it is the usual impression that a big bank is always a strong bank. This impression is to a very great extent correct but strength does not as a universal rule follow bigness. There are certain inevitable impacts on the efficiency of the Bank as a credit house and as a "solvency meeter." consequent upon the increase in size, which retard the progressive building up of good business. Sir Charles Addis who is a great authority on finance and banking and who was also a member of the Babington Smith Indián Currrency Committee of 1919 writing in the Edinburg Review (1918) says:—

> "The bigger the bank, the greater the danger that with the lapse of time it will become intrenched in a bed of vested interests, inimical to change, discountenancing introduction of new ideas and discouraging more efficient methods of young and vigorous competitors."

Of course as credit is a '*sine qua non*' of banking and confidence in the integrity of the bank's position the chief safeguard and condition of the bank's business, so long as the public holds the view, "big bank, strong bank", size means an advantage. It confers prestige and adds to preserve that indefinable and elusive quality--confidence.

The second shortlived idea that the public generally obtains is that a big bank means increased accommodation to commercial and trading houses. This is quite erroneous as the latter find in practice. In the matter of advances a large bank does not give the same accommodation in *toto* as the smaller banks did before amalgamation. Mr. Hartley Withers gives the instance that a firm might be receiving advance of £10,000 from each of the two small banks, but when they combine the amalgamated bank may not consider the firm good enough for an advance of £20,000. On the face of it, "it looks absurd" says Mr. Withers, but he explains it by saying that "such is the psychology of the bank-managing mind." And we find in this illustration the chief reason why the Money Market and the Stock Exchanges are always opposed to banking combinations.

We might also consider in this connection a few general objections raised against amalgamations. It is said that the policy of concentrating control over the nation's money in fewer hands acts in a detrimental manner as far as trade and industry are concerned. Mr. Arthur Kitson lays the charge that the policy of credit centralisation " has tended to undermine the foundations of American trade and industries and has produced a feeling of insecurity and unrest and engendered a loss of confidence. It has wiped out thousands of small producers and created the great trusts". Mr. Kitson is an eminent living economist but his views are not considered to be classic authority on the subject. He has an odd way of rubbing at the smaller details ignoring the broad principles at work. But there is a great deal of truth in his remarks. So far as the country manager is replaced by a man from the Head Office, the bank loses the knowledge, experience and civic pride of a local man. Even if the latter is retained he is not the ideal man for Central Board whose chief desire is to see local overdrafts and advances reduced to a minimum. There is also the great danger of pooling such a big money power in the hands of the few. The shadows of monopoly get too near and when a Government decides to place such stupendous power in the hands of the few it is understood that drastic provisions are made to safeguard the interests of the public. The real danger of big Banks is the threat of monopoly in a very delicate but vital sphere. Mr. Kitson's remarks about amalgamations in English banking are very pertinent :—

> "The system of central control may prove beneficial in the hands of an able and broadminded banker like (the late) Sir Edward Holden . . . but if however this control happens to be exercised by a man who thinks otherwise (than supplying local needs) or whose interests are abroad what is to prevent his denuding the country of money and loaning it to foreign rivals as has been done to a considerable extent in the past?"

This query gives us the key to the at times incomprehensible opposition offered to the amalgamation of the Presidency Banks in India by the Bombay Indian commercial circles. They are reasonably afraid of the pooled strength and power thus obtained over the finances of the country being used for the exploitation of Indian resources to the benefit of British circles only. They suspect that the sectional prejudice against accommodating Indian houses, so far perhaps curbed and circumscribed to a certain extent by local influences, will now find an ample play and "orders from Central Board" will serve for excuses to defer meeting the claims of the Indian market. We do not know what modicum of truth there is in these charges. Neither one can safely predict the sort of attitude the new Imperial Bank will adopt. But we may in passing note that the personality of the head, in this case those of the Managing Governors, decides detailed conducts of action and no measure of restrictive control by legislation can effect a change of heart. It would possibly be the better policy for the Bombay houses if they feel grievously prejudiced by this amalgamation, to try and obtain control through the shareholder's register and dictate the composition of the Local Board than attempt to introduce a severer bureaucratic interference in the top management. The commercial houses have a justifiable complaint if banks do not come to their aid because of the political complexion of their heads. A business man always feels hurt if doubt is thrown over his good faith by refusal of accommodation. He feels he has a moral right to the use of the organised accumulated credit, to the pooling of which he or his compatriots contribute a big share. The bank should simply be a "trustee of the wealth and credit of its clients" and should not act with discrimination because of the incidence of British or colour of some of its customers. There is logic in all this but banks are run by human sensitiveness and human prejudice; and psychology of a particular banking institution is a matter of tradition slowly built up. The pioneers of large scale commerce and banking in India were largely Englishmen and they monopolised naturally all the available accommodation from banks. Now in the field of industry and commerce as in many other spheres, the Indian has learnt to stand on level with the Britisher, but the conservatism of the banks persists. There must be some means to break it but surely not an act of legislature.

The business which the Bank is allowed by law to handle and which it is specifically prohibited from touching is contained in Scedule I of the Act (given below). The lines of the new permissions generally follow the old Act of 1876 save a relaxation here and there notably in the case of bills of exchange business and the London office. The old Banks always felt sore regarding the restrictions placed upon them in the way of a direct approach to the London Market. The Imperial Bank has now been allowed to open an office in London—an obvious improvement—but the Bank shall not, "at its London office, open cash credits or keep cash accounts for or receive deposits from any person who is not or has not been, within the three years last preceding, a customer of the Bank or of any of the Presidency Bank at any of its or their branches in India or Ceylon".—(Schedule I of the Imperial Bank of India Act, 1920).

The inauguration of the Imperial Bank of India was not hailed even by its extreme advocates as the dawn of a new era of banking. The Act does little more in itself than pool the balance sheets of the three Presidency Banks and tack on a system of direct Government control in return for a handsome privilege. We have on record a speech of the Hon'ble Finance Member (Mr. Hailey) summarising the benefits that are expected to follow from amalgamation :—

> "We look firstly to see a fuller, wider and more effective use for commercial and industrial purposes of the Government balances ; (2) the extension of actual banking facilities ; (3) diffusion of sound and reliable banking practice ; and (4) the foundation of an institution which while from one point of view will have some of the aspects and functions of a State Bank will from the point of view of banking be a banker's bank."

The point for us to consider here is, are we reasonably satisfied that such hopes as these outlined above will be the probable deductions from the Imperial Bank of India Act? We will take them one by one.

The most important step proposed is in our opinion the transfer of the keeping of Government Balances to the Imperial Bank. The ultimate abolition of Reserve treasuries is promised and this will put an end to the anomaly of two sorts of banking reserves in the country. It is suggested that the Imperial Bank with the Government Balances at its disposal will greatly minimise the seasonal fluctuations of the Indian discount rate, that the meaningless system of storing away in Treasuries the surplus funds or the Government of India instead of placing them in the market to relieve the stringency will be done away with; that by this transfer some sort of a flexibility will be introduced in the Indian currency. There is no doubt that there is a serious defect in the circulation of money in India. When money goes "up-country" to finance harvests, it does not come back into the city as quickly as it should. This is a serious defect of the Indian market and the incorporation of some elasticity in currency system is sadly needed. But the mere transfer of Cash Balances to the Imperial Bank books will not work the miracle. As a matter of fact they are of least assistance when the market demands are most pressing. It is in the period from October to January or February that the rates jump up and the commercial circles feel the stringency, and it is exactly in the same period that balances are lowest during the year. Mr. Keynes' considered judgment is as follows:—

"Substantial assistance cannot be expected

> from Cash Balances at the time of the year when it is most needed. . . . .for in July the balance generally reaches its highest level. From July onwards until December the revenue collections are comparatively small and the balances steadily go down till they reach their minimum level in November or December."

In the period from January to March, land tax is gathered in but the collections are countered by heavy payments on account of Council Bills at this time of the year. To expect much relief from this source therefore is futile and we will do well not to stress the fact of transfer of balances to the Imperial Bank as leading directly to the relief of the market.

Responsibility to act as fiscal agents of the Government imposes upon the Bank the duty of reaching the remotest place. The provision made in the Act making it obligatory for the Bank to open 100 branches within five years follows directly from the control given to it over Government funds. The extension of banking facilities thus provided is a condition antecedent to the disposal of Cash Balances of the Government. The spread of credit facilities should prove an unmixed blessing. India has not known a banking habit, though sowcars and shroffs have haunted the back streets of Indian towns and villages from time immemorial, and the grip of the local moneylender over the peasantry is perniciously strong. Through extension of banking facilities we will achieve double purposes. For it is a recorded fact that where rural credit banks have granted facilities to the ryot there has been a tendency on the part of the ousted local Marwari to send his surplus money to the bank. We relieve the ryot of his vicious dependence upon the Kaya and the man with riches is taught the secure beneficence of legitimate banking.

The third hope raised by the Hon'ble Finance Member is a pious wish. Education in banking is not a schoolman's task and with all good faiths we cannot turn out a banking expert by intensive culture on the desk. Banking is a profession and an art which one learns by constant practice and experience. The increase in the number of banking houses will '*pro tanto*' require an increased expert staff and the demand for such will provide enough stimulus to young minds to devote themselves to a profession which holds out a bigger number of chances. There have been few Indian bankers because the demand for them has been very poor; the imported material was always preferred because it was better and we didn't require much of it. Now a policy of extension of credit facilities is avowedly to be worked out, the knowledge of banking practice will spread and with increased chances for a career, able men will be attracted to the profession.

Mr. Hailey's final argument was the invocation of the vision of a great State Bank subserving the needs of the public and the banks equally efficiently. As a State Bank we expect the Imperial Bank of India will gradually attain to the standard and the responsibilities of the German Reichsbank. A writer in the "*Capital*" put in thus: the bank is "placed on an inclined plane gathering functions" on the way as it garners more experience and better virtues. The great benefit that will be in the power of the Imperial Bank to confer upon the widely scattered money markets of India is a continuous reduction of remittance charges from one part of the country to another. Extensive collection facilities ought to enable a proportionate reduction of rates until we arrive at the stage where no charge need be made for transfers, as is the practice in England.

As Banker's bank its main duty lies in insuring maintenance and smooth working of the credit system. It is the abnormal times that test the strength of the machinery and in the greater enduring power of a centralised mechanism the chief merits of such amalgamations as those of the three Presidency Banks lie. "Somewhere in every banking system," says Prof. Sprague, "a reserve of cash and of lending power is needed to meet occasions when the banks find themselves confronted with unusual demands for money and loans;" and it is the system of centralised banking with one towering institution commanding large reserves against small credit liabilities, which has worked out to be most beneficent and economical.

A smooth working of the credit system demands control over the discount market. The Indian bank rates have hitherto acted as barometers for record of money pressure. As mere indixes of registration of the conditions of the money market, their usefulness has been very limited. It is expected that the Imperial Bank with command over Government funds will be able to diminish the fluctuations of bank rate and at the same time control the gold supplies. The bank will find out through practice the most effective method of organising a discount market and increase its sensitiveness to a sharp edge. For we must note that high discount rates are not the cure for inflated credits: they may reduce the internal demand for advances, but they can have very little effect in checking the demand for foreign finance. A sharp sensitiveness in the market to the touch of the Bank rate would facilitate a control over credit inflation which is conditioned by the presence of an active Central Bank.

We have no occasion to discuss the restrictions on the business which the Bank is authorised to do. Practically the Presidency Bank Act of 1876 is confirmed in detail. The notable clause in this connection is the one permitting the Bank "to draw, accept, discount, buy and sell bills of exchange and other negotiable securities." This is a move in the right direction and we have no doubts the practice of the Federal Reserve Board influenced the legislators here to a very great extent. Commercial paper has come to be recognised as the ideal bill for banks and the practice in India is no exception. American Federal Reserve Act 1914 restricted discounting to commercial paper only, though the rigidity has since then been relaxed. The Reichsbank also deals very largely in export bills. We think it is a wholesome and beneficial innovation in the Imperial Bank of India Act and we are quite sure that while the relief and facility to trade and commerce will be considerably increased, the organisation of an up-to-date Discount Market will be brought nearer completion.

We have finished our sketchy survey of the new dispensation in the Indian banking world. The future is in the womb of time and prophecy is almost inaptly futile in spheres where psychology and speculation play a prominent part. We may not bless the new regime for we may be genuinely frightened of the stupendous monopoly thus created; but we may not regret the concomitant, though in this opinion incidental, blessings that a monopoly wisely worked may bring.

PART I.

Business which the Bank is authorised to carry on and transact.

The Bank is authorised to carry on and transact the several kinds of business hereinafter specified, namely :—

(*a*) the advancing and lending money, and opening cash-credits upon the security of—

(*i*) stocks, funds and securities, other than immoveable property, in which a trustee is authorised to invest trust money by any Act of Parliament or by any Act of the Governor-General in Council and any securities of a Local Government or the Government of Ceylon;

(*ii*) such securities issued by State-aided railways as have been notified by the Governor General in Council under section 36 of the Presidency Banks Act, 1876, or may be notified by him under this Act in that behalf;

(*iii*) debentures or other securities for money issued under the authority of any Act of a legislature established in British India by, or on behalf of, a district board;

(*iv*) goods which, or the documents of title to which, are deposited with, or assigned to, the Bank as security for such advances, loans or credits;

(*v*) accepted bills of exchange and promissory notes endorsed by the payees and joint and several promissory notes of two or more persons or firms unconnected with each other in general partnership; and

(*vi*) fully paid shares and debentures of companies with limited liability, or immoveable property or documents of title relating thereto as collateral security only where the original security is one of those specified in sub-clauses (*i*) to (*iv*), and if so authorised by any general or special directions of the Central Board, where the original security is of the kind specified in sub-clause (*v*):

Provided that such advances and loans may be made, if the Central Board thinks fit, to the

Secretary of State for India in Council, without any specific security;

(*b*) the selling and realisation of the proceeds of sale of any such promissory notes, debentures, stock-receipts, bonds, annuities, stock, shares, securities or goods which, or the documents of title to which, have been deposited with, or assigned to, the Bank as Security for such advances, loans or credits, or which are held by the Bank, or over which the Bank is entitled to any lien or charge in respect of any such loan or advance or credit or any debt or claim of the Bank, and which have not been redeemed in duetime in accordance with the terms and conditions (if any) of such deposit or assignment;

(*c*) the advancing and lending money to Courts of Wards upon the security of estates in their charge or under their superintendence, and the realisation of such advances or loans and any interest due thereon, provided that no such advance or loan shall be made without the previous sanction of the Local Government concerned, and that the period for which any such advance or loan is made shall not exceed six months;

(*d*) the drawing, accepting, discounting, buying and selling of bills of exchange and other negotiable securities payable in India, or in Ceylon; and, subject to the general or special directions of the Governor General in Council, the discounting and buying of bills of exchange, payable outside India, for and from such Banks as the Governor General in Council may approve in that behalf.

(*e*) the investing of the funds of the Bank upon any of the securities specified in sub-clauses *i* to *iii* of clause *a* and converting the same into money when required, and altering, converting and transposing such investments above specified;

(*f*) the making, issuing and circulating of bank-post-bills and letters of credit made payable in India, or in Ceylon, to order, or otherwise than to the bearer on demand;

(*g*) the buying and selling of gold and silver whether coined or uncoined;

(*h*) the receiving of deposits and keeping cash-accounts on such terms as may be agreed on;

(*i*) the acceptance of the charge of plate, jewels, title-deeds or other valuble goods on such terms as may be agreed up on;

(*j*) the selling and realising of all property whether moveable or immoveable, which may in any way come into the possession of the Bank in satisfaction or part satisfaction of any of its claims;

(*k*) the transacting of pecuniary agency business on commission;

(*l*) the acting as administrator or trustee for the purpose of winding up estates, or the acting as agent on commission in the transaction of the following kinds of business, namely:—

1. the buying, selling, transferring and taking charge of any securities, or any shares in any public Company;

2. the receiving of the proceeds, whether principal, interest or dividends, of any securities or shares;

3. the remittance of such proceeds at the risk of the principal by public or private bills of exchange, payable either in India or elsewhere;

(*m*) the drawing of bills of exchange and the granting of letters of credit payable out of India, for the use of principals for the purpose of the remittances mentioned in clause (*l*) and also for private constituents for *bona fide* personal needs;

(*n*) the buying, for the purpose of meeting

such bills or letters of credit, of bills of exchange payable out of India; at any usance not exceeding six months;

(*o*) the borrowing of money in India for the purposes of the bank's business, and the giving of security for money so borrowed by pledging assets or otherwise;

(*p*) the borrowing of money in England for the purposes of the Bank's business upon the security of the assets of the Bank, but not otherwise and

(*q*) generally, the doing of all such matters and things as may be incidental or subsidiary to the transacting of the various kinds of business hereinfore specified.

PART II

Business which the Bank is not authorised to carry out or transact

The Bank shall not transact any kind of banking business other than those specified in Part I and in particular—

1. It shall not make any loan or advance—

(*a*) for a longer period than six months, or

(*b*) upon the security of stock or shares of the Bank, or

(*c*) save in the case of the estates specified in clause (*c*) of Part I, upon mortgage or in any other manner upon the security of any immoveable property, or the documents of title relating thereto.

2. The Bank shall not (except upon a security of the kinds specified in sub-clauses (*i*) to (*iv*) of clause (*a*) of Part I discount bills for any individual or partnership firm for an amount exceeding in the whole at any one time such sum as may be prescribed or lend or advance in any way to any individual or partnership-firm an amount exceeding in the whole at any one time such sum as may be so prescribed.

3. The Bank shall not discount or buy, or advance and lend, open cash-credits on the security of any negotiable instrument of any individual or partner-ship firm, payable in the town or at the place where it is presented for discount, which does not carry on it the several responsibilities of at least two persons or firms unconnected with each other in general partnership.

4. The Bank shall not discount or buy, or advance and lend, or open cash-credits on the security of any negotiable security having at the date of the proposed transaction a longer period to run than six months or, if drawn after sight, drawn for a longer period than six months:

Provided that nothing in this Part shall be deemed to prevent the *Bank* from allowing any person who keeps an account with the Bank to overdraw such account, without security, to such extent as may be prescribed.

APPENDIX

A Comparative Summary of Conclusions of the

BABINGTON SMITH COMMITTEE OF 1919

1. It is desirable to restore stability to the rupee and to re-establish the automatic working of the Indian currency system.
2. The reduction of the fineness or the weight of the Rupee, the issue of 2 or 3 Rupee coins of lower proportional silver content than the present Rupee, or the issue of a nickel Rupee are expedients that can not be recommended.

   If the legal tender limit of one rupee for the 8 anna nickel coin should prove an obstacle to its free circulation the question of raising the limit to Rs. 5 or Rs. 10 should be considered.
3. The maintenance of the convertibility of the note issue is essential, and proposals that do not adequately protect the Indian paper currency from the risk of becoming inconvertible cannot be entertained.

B

Reports of the two Committees of 1919 and 1914

CHAMBERLAIN COMMISSION OF 1914

(i) The establishment of the exchange value of the rupee on a stable basis has been and is of the first importance to India.

SMITH COMMITTEE—(*continued*)

4. The rise in exchange, in so far as it has checked and mitigated the rise in Indian prices has been to the advantage of the country as a whole, and it is desirable to secure the continuance of this benefit.
5. Indian trade is not likely to suffer any permanent injury from the fixing at a high level.

   If contrary to expectation, a great and rapid fall in world prices were to take place, and if the costs of production in India were to fail to adjust themselves with equal rapidity to the lower level of prices, then it might be necessary to consider the problem afresh.
6. The developement of Indian industry would not be seriously hampered by a high rate of exchange.
7. The gain to India of a high rate of exchange for meeting the Home charges is an incidental advantage that must be taken into consideration.
8. To postpone fixing a stable rate of exchange would be open to serious criticism and entail prolongation of government control.
9. The balance of advantage is decidedly on the side of fixing the exchange value of the rupee in terms of gold rather than in terms of sterling.

CHAMBERLAIN COMMISSION—(*continued*)

(iv) The time has now arrived for a reconsideration of the ultimate goal of the Indian Currency System. The belief of the Committee of 1898 was that a gold currency in active circulation is an essential condition of the maintenance of the Gold Standard in India, but the history of the last 15 years shows

SMITH COMMITTEE--(*continued*)

10. The stable relation to be established between rupee and gold should be at the rate of Rs. 10 to one sovereign, or in other words, at the rate of one rupee for 11. 30016. grains of fine gold, both for foreign exchange and for internal circulation.

11. If silver rises for more than a brief period above the parity of 2s. (gold) the situation should be met by all other available means rather than by impairing the convertibility of the note issue. Such measures might be (*a*) reduction of sale of Council bill (*b*) abstention from purchase of silver; (*c*) use of gold to meet demands for metallic currency. If it should be absolutely necessary to purchase silver, the government should be prepared to purchase even at a price such that rupees would be coined at a loss.

12. Council drafts are primarily sold not for the convenience of trade, but to provide for the Home Charges in the widest sense of the term.

There is no obligation to sell draft to meet trade demands; but if without inconvenience or with advantage the Secretary of State is in a position to sell drafts in excess of his immediate needs, when a trade demand for

CHAMBERLAIN COMMISSION—(*continued*)

that the Gold Standard has been firmly secured without this condition.

(x) The essential point is that this internal currency should be supported for exchange purposes by a thoroughly adequate reserve of gold and sterling.

(xxix) The Secretary of State sells Council drafts, not for the convenience of trade, but to provide the funds needed in London to meet the requirements of the Secretary of State on India's behalf.

SMITH COMMITTEE—(*continued*)

them exists, there is no objection to his doing so, subject to due regard being paid to the principles governing the location of the reserves.

Council drafts should be sold as now by open tender at competitive rates a minimum rate being fixed from time to time on the sterling cost of shipping gold to India. At present this rate will vary; but when sterling is again equivalent to gold, it will remain uniform.

13. The Government of India should be authorised to announce, without previous reference to the Secretary of State on each occasion, their readiness to sell weakly a stated amount Reverse Councils (including telegraphic transfers) during periods of exchange weakness at a price based on the cost of shipping gold from India to the United Kingdom.

14. The quantity of gold taken by India for all purposes in the period before the war was not disproportionately large having regard to her social customs and economic position; but more productive methods for employing wealth should be encouraged.

15. The import and export of gold to and from

CHAMBERLAIN COMMISSION—(*continued*)

(xxx) The India Office perhaps sold Council drafts unnecessarily at very low rates on occasions when the London balance was in no need of replenishment, but we do not recommend any restrictions upon the absolute discretion of the Secretary of State as to the amount of drafts sold or the rate at which they are sold, provided that it is within the gold points. The amount and the occasion of sales should be fixed with reference to the urgency of the Government's requirements and the rate of exchange obtainable whether the drafts are against Treasury balances or against the Reserves.

(xvi) The Government should definitely undertake to sell bills in India on London at the rate of 1s. 3d. and 29/32d. per rupee whenever called upon to do so.

(vi) The people of India neither desire nor need any considerable amount of gold for circulation as currency, and the currency most generally suitable for the internal needs of India consists of rupees and notes.

SMITH COMMITTEE—(*continued*)

India should be free from Government control.

16. The Government should continue to aim at giving the people the form of currency which they demand, whether rupees, notes or gold; but gold can be employed to the best advantage in the Government reserves, where it is available for meeting the demand for foreign remittance.

It would not be to India's advantage actively to encourage the increased use of gold in the internal circulation, but it may be for sometime difficult to meet all demands for metallic currency in rupees, and a more extensive use of gold may be necessary. In order that confidence may not be disturbed by exceptional issues, the issue of gold coin in moderate quantities should be one of the normal methods of meeting demands for currency.

17. The Bombay Branch of the Royal Mint should be re-opened for the coinage of sovereigns and half-sovereigns and facilities should be afforded to the public for the coinage of gold bullion and for the refining of gold.

18. The obligation of the Government to give rupees for sovereigns should be withdrawn.

CHAMBERLAIN COMMISSION—(*continued*)

(vi) See above.

(ix) The Government should continue to aim at giving the people the form of currency which they demand, whether rupees, notes or gold, but the use of notes should be encouraged.

(v) It would not be to India's advantage to encourage an increased use of gold in the internal circulation.

(vii) A Mint for the coinage of gold is not needed for purposes of currency or exchange, but if Indian sentiment genuinelly demands it and the Government of India are prepared to incur the expense, there is no objection in principle to its establishment either from the Indian or from the Imperial standpoint:

SMITH COMMITTEE—(*continued*)

19. Opportunities should be afforded to the public to exchange sovereigns in their possession at the rate of 15 rupees per sovereign at the time of the introduction of the new ratio. Similar opportunities should be given to holders of the gold mohur which should eventually be demonetised.

20. The prohibition on the import of silver should be removed as soon as is convenient.

21. When the prohibition on the import of silver is removed the import duty should also be removed, unless the fiscal position demands its retention.

22. The prohibition on the export of silver should be retained for the present with a view to the protection of silver currency from depletion by export.

If the silver mines in India should cease to be purchased by the Government, its export should be permitted under license.

23. Improved banking facilities and increased opportunities for investment of savings should be afforded.

CHAMBERLAIN COMMISSION—(*continued*)

provided that the coin minted is the sovereign (or the half-sovereign); and it is preeminently a question in which Indian sentiment should prevail.

(viii) If a mint for the coinage of gold is not established, refined gold should be received at the Bombay mint in exchange for currency.

(xli) We are not in aposition to report either for or against the establishment of a State or Central Bank, but we regard the subject as one which deserves early and careful consideration, and suggest the appointment of a small expert committee to examine the whole question in India, and either to pronounce

SMITH COMMITTEE—(*continued*)

24. No recommendation is made for modifying the present practice regulating the purchase of silver for coinage.

25. The statutary minimum for the metallic portion of the Paper Currency Reserve should be 40% of the gross circulation.

As regards the fiduciary portion of the reserve, the holding of securities issued by the Government of India should be limited to 20 crores. The balance should be held in securities of other governments comprised within the British Empire, and of the

CHAMBERLAIN COMMISSION—(*continued*)

against the proposal or to work out in full detail a concrete scheme capable of immediate adoption.

(xxxiii) There is no ground for the suggestion that the City members of the Secretary of state's Council showed any kind of favouritism in placing on deposit with certain banks, with the directorates of which they were connected, a part of the India Office balance at a time when it was too large to be placed entirely with the approved borrowers. But we call the attention of the Secretary of State to the desirability of avoiding as far as possible all occassion for such criticism, though it may be founded on prejudice and ignorance of facts.

(xvii) The Paper Currency system of India should be made more elastic. The fiduciary portion of the note issue should be increased at once from 14 to 20 crores, and thereafter fixed at a maximum of the amount of notes held by Government in the Reserve Treasuries *plus* one-third of the net circulation, and the government should take power to make temporary investments or loans from the

SMITH COMMITTEE—(*continued*)

amount so held not more than 10 crores should have more than one year's maturity, and all should be redeemable at a fixed date. The balance of the invested portion above these 30 crores should be held in short-dated securities, with not more than one year's maturity, issued by governments within the British Empire.

The existing permissive maximum of 120 crores should be retained for a limited period.

The sterling investments and gold in the Paper Currency Reserve should be re-valued at 2s. to the rupee. The depreciation which will result from this re-valuation cannot be made good at once, but any savings resulting from the rise in exchange will afford a suitable means for discharging this liability in a number of years.

26. With a view to meeting the seasonal demand for additional currency provision should be made for the issue of notes up to five crores over and above the normal fiduciary issue as loans to the Presidency banks on the security of export bills of exchange.

27. The silver and gold in the Paper Currency

CHAMBERLAIN COMMISSION—(*continued*)

fiduciary portion within this maximum in India and in London, as an alternative to investment in permanent securities.

(xxiv) The independent Treasury system of the Indian government is not an ideal one. It is partly responsible for the stringency which recurs annually in the Indian Money markets.

(xxv) We recommend that the Government of India should make a regular practice of granting loans to the Presidency Banks from their surplus balances in India against security on

SMITH COMMITTEE—(*continued*)

Resreve should be held in India except for transitory purposes.

28. As soon as circumstances permit, free facilities for the encashment of notes should be given, and the restrictions imposed during the war should be withdrawn. The Government should have the option of redeeming its notes in full legal tender gold or silver coin.

29. No limit can yet be fixed to the amount up to which the gold Standard Reserve should be accumulated, and when profits again accrue on the coinage of rupees they should be credited in their entirety to the reserve.

30. Under present conditions Government should hold such gold as they obtain in the Paper Currency Reserve rather than in the Gold Standard Reserve. The Gold Standard should when practicable contain a considerable proportion of gold; but the most satisfactory course at present lies in keeping the reserve as liquid as possible by the holding of securities with early dates of maturity. The amount of securities in the Reserve with a maturity exceeding three years should not be increased, and the aim should be to hold

CHAMBERLAIN COMMISSION—(*continued*)

terms to be negotiated with the Presidency Banks.

(xviii) We recommend the immediate universliasation of the 500-rupee note and the increase of the facilities for the encashment of notes.

(xi) No limit can at present be fixed to the amount up to which the gold Standard Reserve should be accumlated.

(xii) The profits on coinage of rupees should for the present continue to be credited exclusively to the Reserve.

(xiii) A much larger proportion of the Reserve should be held in actual gold. By an exchange of assets between this reserve, and the Paper Currency Reserve, a total of about £10,000,000 in gold can be at once secured. This total should be raised as opportunity offers to £15,000,000 and thereafter the authorities should aim at keeping one-half of the total Reserve in actual gold.

(xiv) The Indian branch of the Gold Standard Reserve in which rupees are now held should be abolished, the rupees being handed over

SMITH COMMITTEE—(*concluded*)

all the invested portion of the reserve in securities issued by Governments within the British Empire (other than the Government of India) and having a fixed date of maturity of not more than 12 months.

31. A portion of the gold in the Gold Standard Reserve, not exceeding one-half, should be held in India; the sterling investments should continue to be held in London.

CHAMBERLAIN COMMISSION—(*concluded*)

to the Paper Currency Reserve in exchange for gold.

(xv) The proper place for the location of the whole of the Gold Standard Reserve is London.

(xxvi). In deciding upon the location of surplus balances, the Government of India and the Secretary of State should act in consultation, and, while the transmission of the necessary funds to London at favourable rates exchange is the first consideration, the authorities should have regard to all the factors including the possibility of utilising surplus balances for loans in India.

MR. D. M. DALAL'S MINORITY REPORT CONCLUSIONS, 1919

(*a*) The money standard in India should remain unaltered; that is, the standard of the sovereign and gold mohurs with rupees related thereto at the ratio of 15 to 1.

(*b*) Free and unfettered imports and exports by the public of gold bullion and gold coins.

(*c*) Free and unfettered imports and exports by the public of silver bullion and silver coins.

(*d*) The gold mint at Bombay to be continued and to receive gold bullion from the public and to coin free of charge gold mohurs of the same exact weight and fineness as the sovereign and to hand them over to the tenderers of gold bullion in less than 15 days.

(*e*) The Bombay mint to undertake refining of raw gold for the public and not to make any profit on the transaction.

(*f*) The existing silver rupees of 165 grains of fine silver at present in circulation to continue full legal tender.

(*g*) As long as the price of silver in New York is over 92 cents Government should not manufacture silver rupees containing 165 grains fine silver.

(*h*) As long as the price of silver is over 92 cents Government should coin 2-rupee silver coins of reduced fineness compared with that of the present silver rupee and the same to be unlimited legal tender.

(*i*) Government to coin a new 8 anna silver piece of reduced fineness and the same to be unlimited legal tender.

(*j*) Government not to coin an 8-anna nickel piece.

(*k*) Government to sell Council bills by competitive tenders for the amount defined in the Budget as required to be remitted to the Secretary of State. The Budget estimate to show under separate headings the amount of Council bills drawn for Home Charges, for Capital Outlay, and Discharge of Debt. Council bills to be sold for Government requirements only and not for trade purposes, except for the purpose mentioned in the next succeeding recommendation.

(*l*) "Reverse" drafts on London to be sold only at 1s. 3-29/32d. The proceeds of "Reverse" drafts to be kept apart from all other Government funds and not to be utilised for any purpose except to meet drafts drawn by the Secretary of State at a rate not below 1s. 4-3/32d. per rupee.

(*m*) Currency notes should be printed in India.

(*n*) Government not to interfere with the immemorial practice of the Indian public of melting current coins.

(*o*) The sterling investments held against the Indian note issue to be liquidated as early as possible and transmitted to India in gold.

(*p*) The use of one-rupee currency notes to be discontinued as early as possible and meanwhile not to be forced into circulation.

INDEX